APHRODISIAS

A GUIDE TO THE SITE AND ITS MUSEUM

KENAN T. ERİM

NET
TURİSTİK YAYINLAR
SANAYİ VE TİCARET A.Ş.

Born in Istanbul, Kenan T. Erim left Turkey at a very young age, when his father was appointed to the League of Nations in Geneva. He attended primary school and the Collège de Genève there. Following world war II, as his father assumed new duties at the United Nations in New York, he enrolled at New York University, where he completed a B.A. in Classics in 1953. His graduate studies continued at Princeton University, and he obtained an M.A. and Ph.D in Classical Archaeology from that institution in 1955 and 1958. His participation in the Princeton Archaeological Expendition to Sicily, directed by Professors Erik Sjöqvist and Richard Stillwell, afforded him the unique opportunity to discover through his dissertation that the ancient name of the site that was being excavated was Morgantina. Kenan Erim's academic career began at Indiana University (1958), then continued at New York University, his alma mater, where he is presently Professor of Classics.

It was during his studies at Princeton that his interest in Aphrodisias and its sculpture was arused Therefore, as soon as he joined the Faculty of New York University, he started to plan archaeological investigations there and thus hoped to contribute to the archaeology of his native country. Following

KENAN T. ERİM

a preliminary visit to the site in 1959, he organised an expedition in 1961. As Director of the Aphrodisias Excavations ever since, he has conducted regular summer campaigns in the city of Aphrodite with several dedicated collaborators. The brillant results achieved over twenty years are eloquent proofs of the importance of the Aphrodisias project, and have attracted international interest. Beside teaching and researching, Kenan Erim divides his time between fund-raising for Aphrodisias (the National Geographic Society supported his work for many years) and excavating each summer at the site. He has also lectured widely in North America and Europe. He has received many honours and awards that have been bestowed on him for his work at Aphrodisias, including the Liberty Medal Award of New York City in 1986 and the title Commendatore of the Order of Merit of the Republic of Italy in 1987. More recently, he was the recipirent of a National Geographic Society Centennial Award and was cited for his work by the Association for the Promotion of Turkey (Türkiye Tanıtma Vakfı).

Kenan T.Erim, died in the 3rd of November 1990. His grave is in Aphrodisias .

Published and distributed by:
NET TURİSTİK YAYINLAR A.Ş.

Şifa Hamamı Sok. No. 18/2, 34400 Sultanahmet-İstanbul/Turkey
Tel. (90-212) 516 32 28 - 516 82 61 Fax. (90-212) 516 84 68

236. Sokak No.96/B Funda Apt., 35360 Hatay/İzmir/Turkey
Tel. (90-232) 428 78 51   450 69 22 Fax. (90-232) 250 22 73

Kışla Mah., 54. Sok., İlteray Apt., No.11/A-B, 07040 Antalya/Turkey
Tel. (90-242) 248 93 67 - 243 14 97 Fax. (90-242) 248 93 68

Eski Kayseri Cad., Dirikoçlar Apt. No.45, 50200 Nevşehir/Turkey
Tel. (90-384) 213 30 89 - 213 46 20 Fax. (90-384) 213 40 36

Text: **Kenan. T. Erim**
Photographs: **M. Ali Döğenci**
Jonathan S. Blair, Figs. 4,6,12,31 and 33;
David L. Brill, Abb. 48,49 and Restoration Drawing by Robert W. Nicholson
and Michael Hampshire, Fig. 10: all National Geographic Society;
Fig. 5, Courtesy Prof. J. Balty.
Layout: **Not Ajans**
Typesetting: **AS & 64 Ltd. Şti.**
Colour separation: **Asır Matbaacılık Ltd. Şti.**
Printed in Turkey by: **Asır Matbaacılık Ltd. Şti.**

ISBN 975-479-063-9

5th Edition, 1998

CONTENTS

To the Attention of Readers and Visitors:

As outlined in this guide-book, the site of Aphrodisias essentially consists of the remains of the ancient city, excavated or not yet brought to light, and of a museum. During summer and early autumn months, excavation, restoration, and publication preparation activities, accelerated in recent years, are continuing. Because of the demands of such work, it may not always be possible nor safe for the visitor to examine all areas discussed here. Furthermore, due to the limited space provided by the museum, a number of sculpture items and artifacts illustrated in these pages cannot be exhibited. Changes may also occur in some of the museum displays. Plans to remedy to this and, more specifically to transform the whole of Aphrodisias into an archaeological park featuring both indoor and outdoor exhibits and including additional monumental restorations of buildings and approriate sculptural decoration *in situ* are currently being studied.

Introduction

L ong neglected or known only to specialists, the archaeological wealth of Turkey and the significance of Anatolia through centuries and millenia are rapidly attracting the attention that they justly deserve both from scholars and travellers. The unique character of archaeology in Turkey is its variety and quality whatever culture, civilisation or period may be involved.

Of all the innumerable classical sites that dot the landscapes of Anatolia, Aphrodisias ranks unquestionably high among the most subtly beautiful and yet arresting in its atmosphere. Situated about 230 kms. from İzmir and the Acgean coast, Aphrodisias has been the focus of one of the most significant and prolific archaeological enterprises of this century. The exploration of this remarkable site, conducted since 1961 under the aegis of New York University, has yielded many important discoveries, including an unprecedented array of handsome, well-preserved buildings and quantities of splendid sculpture from the Graeco-Roman period. Thanks to its excellent neighbouring marble supplies, and a group of talented and enterprising artists, Aphrodisias was indeed one of the leading sculpture centres of the Roman world, as well as one of the main cult-places dedicated to the goddess Aphrodite, from whom it derived its name. Nowhere else, not only in Anatolia but also in the entire Mediterranean basin, can the flavour of a "school" of sculptors, feverishly active on homeground as well as abroad for nearly six centuries (from the first century B.C. to the end of the fifth century A.D.), be better captured. Even after twenty-eight years of excavations and study, Aphrodisias does not cease to produce striking archaeological treasures and perspectives concerning a rich, varied past that can be traced to prehistoric times.

1. View of the Temple of Aphrodite. From an engraving in **Antiquites of Ionia** *(1840), III. Chapter 2, Pl. III.*

Early Excavations

In contrast to ancient cities along the west and southwest coast of Anatolia, the site of Aphrodisias received little attention from visitors or scholars before the later eighteenth and nineteenth centuries. Part of this neglect was probably due to the difficulty of access to its vicinity. From the late 1700's, among those who visited Aphrodisias, sketched, copied inscriptions or drew plans, one must mention the English group of architects and draughtsmen of the Society of Dilettanti, and Charles Texier, who came in 1835. These and other accounts, whether published or not, began to extract Aphrodisias from an undeserved oblivion. In 1892, Osman Hamdi Bey, then Director General of the Imperial Museums in Constantinople, also visited the site and decided to undertake its exploration. However, he was unable to carry out his project. Consequently, when a French engineer,

amateur archaeologist and collector named Paul Gaudin offered to undertake the excavations, he was readily granted permission to start work. His first campaign took place in 1904 and focused on a general survey of the ancient remains and began excavations at several points, including the temple of Aphrodite and particularly a large complex that proved to be the so-called Baths of Hadrian. An unusual amount of architectural and sculptural fragments was unearthed, so that a second campaign was planned, the following year. Although he started its activities, Gaudin had to leave for another assignment in Syria and Arabia, and the work was completed by Gustave Mendel. In 1913, an attempt was made to resume the excavations by André Boulanger, under the aegis of the French School of Athens. The international political situation, however, hindered such a plan. It was only in 1937 that work was resumed at the site by an Italian mission, led

2. Baths of Hadrian.

by Giulio Jacopi, who concentrated his efforts in the vicinity of the Baths of Hadrian and the adjacent agora. But these activities were also cut short by the worsening international situation. On the other hand, several important studies and publications appeared during and immediately after World War II, especially the account of Jacopi's 1937 work and Maria F. Squarciapino's *La scuola di Afrodisia*. The latter proved to be eminently important, as Squarciapino meticulously collected and analysed all evidence relevant to the sculptors of Aphrodisias, including their signatures, and was the first scholar to give credit to the creative abilities of the Carian artists and their contribution to the sculpture of the Graeco-Roman world. Indeed, prior to her study, the Aphrodisian sculptors were regarded as mere copyists of earlier Greek and Hellenistic statuary.

Partly spurred by these publications and by the decision of the Turkish authorities to relocate the village of Geyre that had grown over much of the remains of the ancient city, the present series of investigations was initiated in 1961 under the aegis of New York University, and has continued with regular, annual summer campaigns ever since. The chief aims of the expedition were to survey carefully the site, to explore its history and prehistory by means of excavations in a number of crucial areas and monuments and, more particularly, to document archaeologically the background and development of the activities of Aphrodisian sculptors with fresh and more persuasive evidence. The spectacular results achieved in twenty eight years of work by the New York University mission and

3. Fragment of "peopled scrolls" pillar found in 1904 by P. Gaudin in the Baths of Hadrian (now in the İstanbul Archaeological Museums).

4. Younger magistrate, or **chlamydatus**, found in 1904 by P. Gaudin in front of the Baths of Hadrian (now in the İstanbul Archaeological Museums). Fifth century.

5. Bearded male portrait head. Fifth century. Found in 1904 by P. Gaudin in the underground corridors of the Baths of Hadrian (now in Brussels).

outlined here have more than justified the efforts and interest of all involved in the project, whether scholars, archaeologists or supporters.

6. *Head of a Polykleitan-type athlete from the frieze of the Portico of Tiberius, found in 1937 by G. Jacopi (now in the İzmir Archaeological Museum).*

7. *View of the recently restored north flank of the Portico of Tiberius.*

8. *Portico of Tiberius with architrave bearing part of dedicatory inscription in foreground.*

History of Aphrodisias

As its name suggests, Aphrodisias was named after Aphrodite, goddess of nature, love and fertility, and was the site of one of her most famous sanctuaries. The name 'Aphrodisias', however, came into use rather late, probably in the Hellenistic period (ca. 2nd cent. B.C.). Prior to that, the city, or more accurately the site, seems to have been known by several other names. Ancient texts unfortunately do not provide clear information about its pre-Hellenistic appellation, nor for that matter about its early history or prehistory. Much of what is known today and is summarized below has to be reconstructed from the study and analysis of the abundant archaeological evidence unearthed in recent years.

Most ancient sources reckon Aphrodisias among the cities of Caria, the region comprising the southwestern corner of modern Turkey, although the site is also near the confines of ancient Lydia (to the northwest) and Phrygia (to the northeast). In his catalogue of cities, a late writer, the grammarian Stephanus of Byzantium (ca. sixth cent. A.D.) also lists Aphrodisias as Ninoè, a name derived from Ninos. Ninos, a mythical founder of the Assyro-Babylonian empire and the husband of the famous Semiramis, was purported to be a son of Belos (or Bel, divine equivalent of the Greek Kronos) and the conqueror or much of western Asia as far as the Aegean. It is also worth remembering that the name Ninos was derived from the Akkadian appellations for the Near Eastern goddess, Ishtar (or Astarte), Nin, Ninai, Nana or even Enana, who was also a divinity connected with love and war. Consequently, it is not implausible to suggest that "Aphrodisias" was a Greek translation of Ninoè that came into use in later Hellenistic times (ca. 2nd cent. B.C.) when the local goddess was identified with Aphrodite (and by im-

plication the Roman Venus) and the site became a full-fledged city. Indeed, prior to that time, Aphrodisias must have been a temple or sacred site, including essentially a sanctuary, its dependencies and estates tended to by a reasonably extensive rural population. The adoption of a new name may well have been spurred also by the growing reputation of the cult of the goddess as well as the establishment of a Roman presence in western Asia Minor. As noted above, Aphrodite was naturally the equivalent of the Roman Venus, from whom, furthermore, the Romans claimed descent through her son Aeneas. Aeneas himself was from Trojan stock, that is from northwestern Anatolia, before he set out westward, reached eventually Italy and his descendants founded Rome. In short, the identification of the two goddesses may be regarded as a clever form of political manoeuver and flattery, not uncommon at the time, and one that would eventually prove rewarding to Aphrodisias in the first century B.C.

The cult of the goddess, whatever her early name may have been, must undoubtedly have roots in prehistoric times. For, as revealed by recent excavations, the site was occupied as early as the late Neolithic (?) period, and, after a hiatus, resettled in the late Chalcolithic then developed through the Bronze and Iron Ages (ca. 4360-546 B.C.). The reasonable proximity of the Maeander (mod. Büyük Menderes) river system and its well-watered plain played a significant role in the early growth of the settlement. The archaeological evidence discovered in two artificial, habitation mounds or *höyüks*, the Acropolis and Pekmez hillocks, located in the southern and southeastern areas of the site suggested one or two small villages of essentially agricultural character. The abundant ceramic and artifact collections and other data revealed connections with neighbouring Anatolian and Aegean sites such as Hacilar,

Beycesultan, Kum Tepe, Kusura and Troy. A number of small stone "idols" found in these contexts may even be looked upon as the first manifestations of a divinity that would eventually become the *raison d'être* of the site.

Evidence concerning Aphodisias in the Archaic and Classical periods (seventh-fourth cent. B.C.) lack clear definition, but implies a slow development of the cult of the local goddess in the temple area and by the Acropolis. As already mentioned, the consolidation of Roman rule in Asia Minor in the second century B.C. led to the growth of the sanctuary into a city and the assumption of the name Aphrodisias. The growing reputation of the goddess is echoed in a passage of the historian Appian (2nd cent. A.D.) that states that, during the Mithradatic Wars, in 82 B.C., the Roman dictator Sulla, advised by the oracle at Delphi to honour the Carian Aphrodite, sent her a golden crown and a double axe. At about that same time, the name of Aphrodisias also appears, coupled with that of a neighbouring town, Plarasa (probably mod. Bingçç) on small bronze and silver coins.

Many crucial inscribed documents pertaining to the first century B.C. history of Aphrodisias were discovered in the excavations of the theatre, on the walls of its stage building. One of these refers to a golden statue of Eros dedicated to Aphrodite by Julius Caesar. This, and other inscriptions, suggest that the Roman leader also paid homage to the goddess, perhaps by visiting her sanctuary, and that, after his assassination in 44 B.C., the city was captured and plundered by the men of Labienus, a follower of Caesar's murderers, because of its loyalty to Octavian and Anthony. As a reward for this loyalty, in 39 B.C., Aphrodisias was granted special privileges through a triumviral, a senatorial decree, a treaty as well as a law. This included freedom, a non-taxable status as well as increased asylum rights in Aphrodite's sanc-

9. Portrait head of Julius Caesar. First century B.C.

tuary, according to further documents found in the theatre. The influence wielded by Octavian, Caesar's heir in these decisions, was undoubtedly crucial. In one of his letters found inscribed on the theatre stage building, Octavian referred very warmly to Aphrodisias as well as to Zoilos, an Aphrodisian who was a freedman of his. Such sentiments persisted well after Octavian became the emperor Augustus in 27 B.C. Zoilos, on the other hand, was highly esteemed by his fellow citizens for the role he played in their relationship with Rome and for the many benefactions he bestowed on their city.

From the later first century B.C., Aphrodisias enjoyed a long period of prosperity and renown. The Julio-Claudian emperors were naturally partial to the city. In 22 A.D., Tiberius reconfirmed the privileges granted earlier by the Senate. Subsequent emperors, from Trajan to Gordian III Decius and Herennius Etruscus, continued to show good will through the third century as made clear by in-

10. *Restoration drawing of the core of ancient Aphrodisias in the late second century. By Robert W. Nicholson, and Michael Hampshire.*

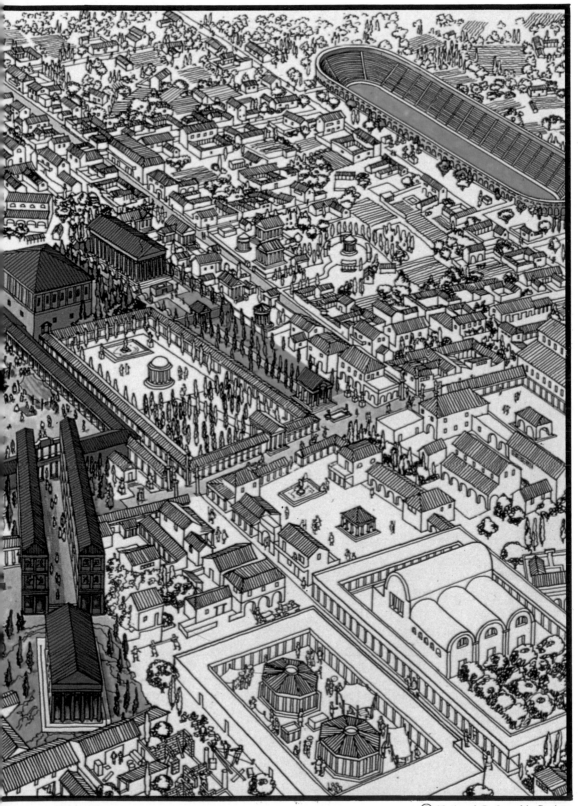

11. "Archive wall". Theatre.

scribed documents found in the theatre. These centuries also witnessed the increasing fame of the cult of Aphrodite that drew visitors and pilgrims from far and wide and, above all, the importance of its school of sculpture. Indeed, already from the first century B.C., spurred by the excellent marble supplies located in the Salbakos mountains (mod. Baba Dağ) immediately northeast of the city, sculptors produced beautiful statuary of all kind, reliefs, portraits, sarcophagi and decorative elements that rapidly came to be in demand in Rome as well as elsewhere in the Mediterranean. In addition, Aphrodisias also fostered literary, scientific and other intellectual pursuits. Xenocrates wrote medical treatises in the first century. Chariton was the author of one of the early romances (or novels) of antiquity (second century) and Alexander was the most able commentator and teacher of the works of the great Aristotle and lectured about them in Athens, in the later second century.

However, the troubled third century saw a gradual change in the status of Aphrodisias, as is the case for many other cities. It became for a while the administrative centre of a combined province of Caria and Phrygia. Subsequently, under the reign of Diocletian (284-305) or shortly thereafter, it was made capital, or metropolis, of a smaller province of Caria. Thereafter, with the gradual division of the Empire into two parts, its fate naturally became bound with that of the Eastern Roman and later the Byzantine Empire. The advent of Christianity in the fourth century led to the establishment of a bishopric, but this did not easily eradicate a deeply rooted pagan past. Two early Christian martyrs were nevertheless ascribed to it, and several of its bishops were deeply involved in the theological disputes and heresies about the nature of Christ that perturbed the early. Christian centuries. Still, pagan philosophy managed to survive at Aphrodisias. Asklepiodotos (from Alexandria), who advocated Neo-Platonism, appears to have bestowed many benefactions on the city in the late fifth century. On the other hand, the new order was intent to wipe out any lingering paganism. The words "Aphrodisias" and "Aphrodisian" were almost systematically erased on most inscriptions. Attempts were even made to impose "Stavropolis" (City of the Cross), as a name for the city around the seventh century. However, "Aphrodisias" did not entirely disappear, but another name "Caria" began to be used in the Byzantine period as it continued to be the chief locality in that area. It is more than probable that the Turkish name of the village of Geyre stems from the Byzantine usage.

Throughout its history, because of its situation in a geologically unstable area, Aphrodisias was affected by many earthquakes. Some that occurred in early Imperial times attested to by either ancient historians or by inscriptions, may have been serious, but their traces are not obvious on the surviving monuments because of successful restoration of their damages. In the fourth century, and thereafter, such natural catastrophes are more readily traceable. In the 350s and the 360s for instance, Aphrodisias was damaged by serious earthquakes like its neighbour Ephesus. The worst effect of these disasters was on the ground water-table of the area, which rose and damaged many of the canalizations of the city that brought water from the eastern mountain slopes. As a result, extensive flooding occurred in the lower lying areas. Many of the damaged buildings were repaired in the fifth century and various, ingenious attempts made to stop the inundations. Subsequent earthquakes may well have exacerbated this problem, particularly a disastrous one that probably occurred in the reign of Heraclius (610-641). Much of its damage, visible in several monuments, was never repaired and ruins left where splendid buildings once stood.

Thus, like many cities of the later Roman, then Byzantine empire, Aphrodisias managed to hold its own and maintained its importance until the seventh century. However, invasions from the east, religious strife, politital and economic pressures, and plagues, hastened its decline. The seventh century earthquake mentioned above was furthermore a terrible blow from which the city never recovered. The fortification system built essentially in the fourth century around the inhabited area could not be restored, nor manned, and, therefore, a stronghold was created circling the hillock of the Acropolis (the former *höyük*) as it was an excellent lookout point for the neighbouring area.

Information regarding Aphrodisias-Caria after the seventh century is limited. There are names of bishops in various patriarchal documents. Archaeologically speaking, a brief revival may be inferred from certain remains datable to the eleventh century. However, bet-

ween that and the thirteenth century, the appearance and eventual establishment of the Seljuk Turks in Anatolia and its western confines doomed most of the remaining urban centres. At least four captures of Caria (*alias* Aphrodisias) are recorded or implied in contemporary Byzantine sources in the twelfth and thirteenth century. After the thirteenth century, the whole area fell within the territory of the *beylik* of Aydın, or of Menteşe. Aphrodisias must have been abandoned. However, in the fifteenth or sixteenth century, the fertility of the plateau attracted settlers again, and eventually, the Turkish village of Geyre grew over and among the ruins of once handsome monuments.

The Site

As already noted, in ancient geographical terms, Aphrodisias is usually considered to be in the region known as Caria, that includes most of southwestern Turkey. Today, it is located in the province (*il*) of Aydın, its district (*ilçe*) of Karacasu, about 230 kms. southeast of the Aegean seaport of Izmir, and on a high, well-watered plateau ca. 600 m. above sea-level. It is framed to the east by the Baba Dağ (ancient Salbakos) range and can be considered part of the Büyük Menderes (ancient Maeander) river system. Indeed, a number of streams descending from the Baba Dağ mountains join waters to form a tributary called today the Dandalas that flows into the Menderes near Başaran (ancient Antioch-on-the-Maeander), not far from where the Karacasu-Aphrodisias branch forks off the Izmir-Denizli main road.

The area of the ancient city is essentially flat with a gentle incline towards the southwest. Its only irregularities are the Acropolis mound, ca. 24 m. high and what remains of the Pekmez hillock which rises ca. 13 m. Until recently the village of Geyre was located directly over the main core of the ancient city. In 1956, however, southwestern Turkey suffered a damaging earthquake. Although Geyre was not much affected, the Turkish authorities decreed that here, as well as in one or two other archaeological sites similarly covered by later settlements, it was appropriate to move these villages to more suitable locations. A new Geyre, therefore, began to be built in the early 1960's about 2 kms. west of the Byzantine walls of Aphrodisias. However, habitation in the village continued well until the late 1970's, when all of its stone cottages were expropriated.

12. *General view of the village of Geyre, looking east, in the early 1960's.*

The Walls, the City Plan and the Temple of Aphrodite

As one approaches Aphrodisias from the direction of Karacasu, after bypassing the road leading to new Geyre to the right, the visitor can observe large portions of still standing walls and soon the Ionic columns of the temple of Aphrodite silhouetted against the abundant poplar groves that grow on the eastern part of the site.

The walls belong to a fortification system, roughly circular in perimeter for about 3.5 kms. and featuring a number of towers and at least four principal gates at the cardinal points. This circuit that encircled the heart of the ancient city, an area of ca. 494 hectares, was essentially built in the fourth century and afterwards. Examination of its remaining sections reveals reuse of much architectural, epigraphical and other material that most likely belonged to structures felled by the fourth century earthquakes or later similar

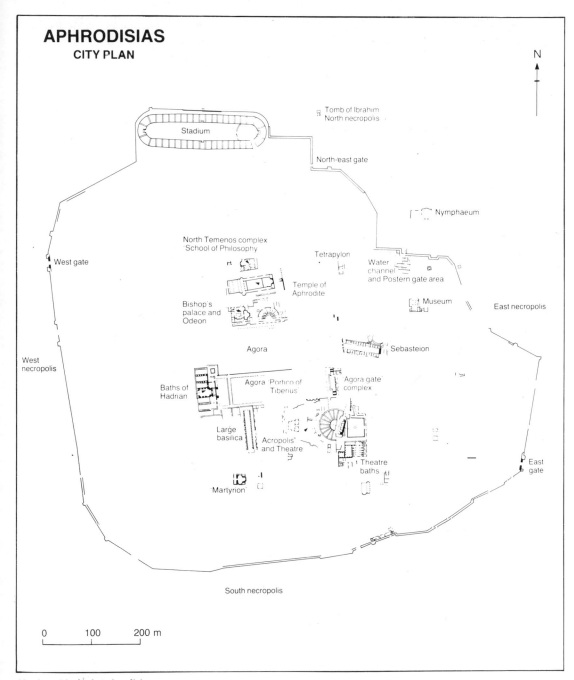

APHRODISIAS
CITY PLAN

N

Stadium

Tomb of Ibrahim
North necropolis

North-east gate

Nymphaeum

West gate

North Temenos complex
School of Philosophy

Tetrapylon

Water channel
and Postern gate area

Temple of Aphrodite

Bishop's palace and Odeon

Museum

East necropolis

Agora

Sebasteion

West necropolis

Baths of Hadrian

Agora Portico of Tiberius

Agora gate complex

Large basilica

Acropolis and Theatre

Theatre baths

East gate

Martyrion

South necropolis

0   100   200 m

13. City Plan of Aphrodisias.

catastrophes. It is possible that the fortification system began to be built in the 260's when Gothic invasions created panic among many western Anatolian cities, but most of the evidence points to a fourth and later centuries construction and repairs. As yet, there is no clear indication of an earlier defence system, but it is possible that something may have been located in Hellenistic times on or near the Acropolis mound, which eventually in the seventh century was indeed transformed into a citadel or stronghold.

14. *Fragment of still standing city wall (Fourth century and after).*

15. *Fragment of still standing city wall (Fourth century and after).*

Because of the severe limitations placed on the early phases of the recent excavations and the slow pace of expropriations, a precise understanding of the growth of the site and eventually its city-plan has been difficult. It is clear, however, from the general plan and the results of excavations that the cores of early habitation were the two prehistoric mounds, their immediate vicinity and the area of the temple of Aphrodite. A more regular "gridiron" development of the site as it turned into a city in the late Hellenistic period is evident in the placing of the agora complex and its neighbourhood. Although a pattern of North-South and East-West streets crossing at right angles seems to be gradually emerging, as excavations continue, it still cannot be said that there was a precise master-plan in the growth of the city. It is, indeed, obvious that several sacred areas, such as the temple of Aphrodite and the *Sebasteion*, did not fit into a regular scheme of habitation blocks.

The temple of Aphrodite, located in the northern half of the site, was the focal point of the city in antiquity, as it still is today with its fourteen standing columns. Unfortunately, the extensive remodelling of the building into a Christian basilica in the late fifth century obscures considerably its early features. The temple was transformed by the removal of its cella walls, where the cult statue stood and the shifting of its front and some of its side columns and the building of walls to the north and south in order to create a nave and two aisles. An apse and an atrium were added to the east and west. The pagan temple was apparently an octastyle structure with thirteen columns on the sides and had been completed under Augustus (not in the second century as suggested prior to recent excavations). The *temenos*, on the other hand, an elaborate precinct, many elements of which were also reused by the Byzantine architect-remodellers, was organised under Hadrian.

16. Temple and **temenos** of Aphrodite.

17. *Temple of Aphrodite at sunset.*

18. *Terracotta figurine of seated goddess. Later sixth century B.C.*

Traces of an earlier structure, undoubtedly a shrine, were also detected in recent soundings. Study of the remains and the recovered pottery and artifacts clearly pertain to a late Archaic period sanctuary. Unfortunately, the Byzantine rebuilders, as some of their predecessors did, obliterated much evidence by reusing and recutting fragments of earlier structures. Equally regrettable was the Byzantine practice to dig tombs in and around the temple-basilica, which destroyed the stratigraphy of the sacred area and scattered much useful evidence. A colossal, but battered, cult-statue of Aphrodite was discovered reused in a Byzantine foundation south of the *temenos*. Though it was not the cult image proper, it was probably set up inside the precinct of the goddess.

19. *Archaic (including "Lydian") small-type pottery. Seventh-sixth century B.C.*

20. *Tetrapylon. From the west.*

21. *Fragment of relief showing Eros among acanthus scrolls. From the decoration of the west pediment of the Tetrapylon.*

The Tetrapylon

East of the temple, one of the most attractive landmarks of Aphrodisias is a decorative gateway datable to the middle of the second century, the *Tetrapylon*. Its specific relationship to the *temenos* is not yet clear. It consisted of four rows of four columns (hence, the word *Tetrapylon*, from the Greek *tetra* = four and *pylon* = gateway), and its main access was from the east, with a front row of attractive, spirally-fluted Corinthian columns facing a main north-south street. A broken pediment with a semicircular lintel was featured between the second and third columns of the first east and west rows, and echoed by a semicircular lunette on the second row. The sides of the broken pediment over the west columns were lavishly decorated with relief

22. *Restoration drawing of the east façade of the* **Tetrapylon** *(Alois Machatschek).*

23. *Restoration drawing of the west façade of the* **Tetrapylon** *(Alois Machatschek).*

24. *Restoration activities in the* **Tetrapylon** *(1987).*

figures of Erotes and Nikes hunting among scrolls of acanthus leaves. Because of its unusually handsome aspects and the availability of the majority of its component parts that were recovered in the course of excavations, the *Tetrapylon* is in process of being discreetly reerected.

As of this writing, its sixteen columns have been repaired and reset on their high plinths, and its entablatures and upper portions partly replaced in their original position work should be completed by 1990.

25. Odeon. General view.

The Odeon and the Bishop's Palace

To the south of the temple of Aphrodite, a very well-preserved concert-hall, or odeon, was discovered accidentally in 1962. It is another striking monument of Aphrodisias. The odeon was once roofed, but its upper tiers of seats collapsed, probably in the course of the fourth century earthquakes. The effects of the inundations caused by that disaster are evident in the orchestra, below the eight preserved rows of seats, where water still manages to seep into the basin created by the removal of perhaps two lower tiers of seats. This measure was taken to allow the waters threatening the foundations of the building to flow into the semicircular pool whence it could be evacuated by hand. An *opus sectile* mosaic decorating the floor of the basin and now removed and in storage was smaller than the semicircular area of the orchestra and left an unpaved border where the ground water could filter into the basin. The edge, or *pulpitum* of the stage, was also affected by these changes, but, fortunately, many of the handsome statues that adorned the niches of its stage complex were found fallen onto its floor or into the orchestra-pit in the excavations and are now displayed in the museum. More intimate than the theatre, though its original capacity when roofed may have been close to a thousand, the odeon witnessed not only concert, ballet, pantomime or music-hall-type performances, but city-council and public lecture meetings.

A backstage corridor opened to the south into a porticoed area decorated with full-length portrait-statues of notable Aphrodisians and connected with the north colonnade of the north portico of the agora complex.

26. Odeon. View showing **opus sectile** mosaic (now in storage) in the orchestra.

27. Restoration drawing in cross-section of the Odeon. Courtesy Dr. G. Izenour.

28. *Circular stepped platform with tomb* **(heroon)** *behind Odeon.*

29. *"Bishop's Palace" 's peristyle court. From the west.*

Nestled against the back of the odeon, to its northwest, a circular stepped platform with a sarcophagus box inserted into its centre was once part of a funerary monument of some local notable. The area to the north of this tomb may once have been occupied by a gymnasium, prior to the construction of the odeon. In the fourth century, however, it was occupied by a sculptors' workshop, judging from the abundant amount of finished and un-finished sculpture fragments recovered here.

To the west of the odeon, an elaborate complex, featuring a triconch, or triapsidal end and an attractive peristyle court (whose blue marble columns were reerected in 1965) as well as several private facilities, was a residence (for a local governor?) in the late Roman period, but was subsequently converted into a palace for the bishop of Aphrodisias.

30. "Bishop's Palace". From the north.

The Stadium

L ocated in the northern end of the city, the stadium is unquestionably a most stunning monument, and probably the best preserved structure of this type in the Mediterranean. It is ca. 262 m. long and 59 m. wide, features two semicircular ex-tremities and could accommodate as many as 30,000 people. Its long sides were intentionally flaring out, giving them a sort of elliptical shape so that spectators seated here would not block each other's view looking towards the semicircular ends. The stadium was used essentially for athletic events, but, after the seventh century earthquake seriously damaged the theatre of the city, its eastern extremi-

31. *Stadium.*

32. *Stadium. Looking west.*

ty was converted for arena games, circus and animal shows. The arcades and walls visible above the tiers of the seats to the northeast formed part of the city's fortification system. Indeed, the stadium was intelligently incorporated into the northern defence system when the walls were built around Aphrodisias, since, if left outside the circuit, it could have been easily used as a point of attack against the city.

The Acropolis and Prehistoric Aphrodisias

The *höyük*, or artificial mound rising to a height of 24 m. and occupying an important position in the southern section of the site, is clearly visible from all approaches. It is, therefore, justifiable to have labelled it "Acropolis" though at its origin it was the core of prehistoric occupation and served as a lookout point only after the seventh century, as already noted. Seven periods related to various phases of the Bronze and Iron Ages, including mudbrick walls on stone foundations and some megaroid architectural features, as well as hearths, storage pits and *pithoi* to hold grain and other foods, were recognised here in trenches dug along the west slope of the hillock. Much characteristic pottery, quantities of artifacts such as loomweights, spindle whorls, stone tools and many stone figurines, or "idols" of the owl-faced, notched-waisted and "fat lady" variety were recovered in the relevant strata. The "Pekmez" mound, on the other hand, the remains of which are located to the east of the Acropolis, yielded earlier assemblages of evidence dating back to the Late Neolithic (?), the Late Chalcolithic and Early Bronze ages, including relevant pottery and two "Kilia" figurines.

33. *Acropolis mound. Prior to the excavations of the theatre in the early 1960's.*

34. *Acropolis mound. Two Bronze Age idols.*

35. *Acropolis mound. Prehistoric investigations on the west slope.*

36. Theatre excavations in course (1971).

The Theatre

In the second half of the first century B.C., the Aphrodisians decided to scoop out the eastern slope of the Acropolis and build a large theatre there. Although several tiers of its upper seats were visible prior to current excavations, this whole side of the hill was covered with a large number of old Geyre stone cottages. The exploration of the Acropolis and the excavation of the theatre were started in 1966 with generous support from the National Geographic Society, and produced crucial evidence for the history, and prehistory, of Aphrodisias as well as a remarkably well-preserved structure and high quality sculpture. In its present form, the theatre betrays a number of repairs and changes brought about in the second century and in Byzantine times. The stage building was obviously damaged in the fourth century earthquakes, restored, then collapsed completely in the seventh century catastrophe. The upper cavea was also seriously affected then and, consequently, the Byzantine inhabitants decided to fill in with débris the ruined and collapsed area of the stage and orchestra, built houses on top of the cavea and, circling the hill with a system of walls and towers, transformed it into a fortress.

The original first century B.C. construction date of the theatre was suggested by a dedication inscribed on the stage building. The *logeion* and *proskenion* of the complex were indeed the gift of G. Julius Zoilos "to Aphrodite and the People (of the city)". Zoilos, mentioned earlier, was a former slave of Octavian, and, therefore, an important link with Rome. He was instrumental, along with others, in obtaining the special status granted to his native Aphrodisias, as a "free and tax-exempt" city. On the inscription of the *proskenion*, he is described as a "freedman of the son of the divine Julius", i.e. Octavian. Since

37. Theatre. Looking north-east.

38. Theatre. Stage with restored **proskenion-logeion**.

34

39. Theatre. **Proskenion-logeion** with dedicatory architrave inscription of Zoilos.

40. Theatre. General view with **conistra** and orchestra arrangement.

41. *Statue of pugilist found on the stage of the Theatre and signed by Polyneikes. Ca. 230 A.D..*

the latter is not yet called Augustus (or in Greek, *Sebastos*), the stage structure was clearly completed before 27 B.C. when he assumed that name.

The stage building, however, must have been originally somewhat different, for it appears to have been tampered with in the second century when the theatre was subjected to important modifications, as indicated by epigraphical and archaeological evidence. The main objective of this work was to transform the structure so that it could be used for the ever popular gladiatorial combats, wrestling bouts, and animal hunts or baitings. The orchestra was, therefore, deepened by removing two or three of the lowest rows of seats and replacing them with a straight supporting wall, thus creating a *conistra* arrangement that protected spectators from the violent activities that took place in the orchestra pit. The stage itself was

42. *"Archive" wall of Theatre in north **parodos** area.*

43. Detail of "archive" wall inscription.

also widened and joined to the cavea and *con-istra*, and under this extension, a system of galleries and corridors was engineered for refuge and animals, with doors acceding to the orchestra. It seems logical that the *proskenion-logeion* unit was at that time also affected by these changes.

The core of the stage building consisted of six vaulted, medium-sized rooms, dressing or storage rooms. Four of these opened unto the corridor behind the *proskenion*, but two communicated with a central barrel-vaulted tunnel that divided the stage building into two. The back portions of these rooms were damaged during the fourth century earthquakes and subsequently repaired. Similar restorations were undertaken in the north stage corridor, or *parodos*, where in the second and third century, a veritable archive of important documents related to the history of

the city were inscribed. Preserved to a height of ca. 5 m. for a length of 15 m., this stage building wall was covered with well-cut inscriptions in Greek. Most of these were letters from Roman leaders and emperors ranging from late Republican times to the middle of the third century, but others were part of the senatorial decree that conferred special status and privileges to Aphrodisias and other documents.

Abundant sculptural decoration from the stage and its façade was recovered from excavations. Among them, a pair of boxers, or pugilists, a symbolic representation of the people of the city in the guise of a handsome young man, an excellent replica of the fifth century B.C. sculptor Polykleitos' *Diskophoros*, Muses and Nikes can now be seen in the musuem.

44. Replica of Polykleitos **Diskophoros**. From the
Theatre.
45. Nike bearing a trophy. From stage decoration of
the Theatre.

The Tetrastoon and Theatre Baths

*T*he changes in the water table and ensuing flooding caused by the later fourth century earthquakes affected the low lying agora area situated immediately to the north base of the Acropolis. While attempting to find a solution to this problem, the Aphrodisians urgently needed a new, centrally situated public area on dry ground. A large "piazza", or *tetrastoon* (as it was called in an inscription found near, since it consisted of four (*tetra*) porticoes (or stoas) on four sides around a roughly square area) was meticulously paved with a round fountain placed at its centre. Even a large round altar was inserted into its pavement and converted into a sundial.

The *tetrastoon* was probably not quite adequate for the needs of the city. Consequently, a hall in basilica plan, the so-called Imperial Hall of the bathing establishment located to the south of the *tetrastoon* was connected with the "piazza" by means of a door opened in the backwall of the niche where a statue of the emperor must have once stood.

Only a portion of these Theatre Baths has been so far excavated and partially restored. The complex appears to extend south and westward along the south slope of the Acropolis. Beside the Imperial Hall, an *apodyterium* (dressing area), a well-preserved circular, domed *calidarium* (or hot bath unit) and a *sudatorium* (sweating room) were fully or partly brought to light here. Most of the columns of the Imperial Hall, carved out of local blue-greyish marble were recovered and restored in their places, as were parts of two elaborately decorated (in the "peopled scrolls" style) pilasters framing the large rectangular niche (or *oecus*) where a statue of the emperor once stood before the opening of the door connecting it with the *tetrastoon*. Shops and boutiques were created in the aisles of the hall.

46. *General view of **tetrastoon** (in foreground) and Theatre Baths (in background).*

47. *Imperial Hall of Theatre Baths. Looking north.*

48. *Detail of "peopled scrolls" pillar of the Imperial Hall of the Theatre Baths.*

49. *Theatre Baths.**Calidarium**, or circular domed hall.*

The Agora

*T*he large public or market area of Aphrodisias was planned in the later first century B.C. and thereafter, in the heart of the city between the Acropolis and the temple of Aphrodite. This agora consisted of two long Ionic porticoes stretching east-west for a length of over 200 m. The northern one of these porticoes has not yet been explored and may have been started earlier than its southern counterpart. Several of its elegant columns, including some forming its southeast corner, are still standing after many centuries among the attractive poplar groves planted by villagers.

The south portico, better known as Portico of Tiberius, has been more systematically explored since earlier excavations. Indeed, it was

50. *General view of Agora.*

51. *North portico of Agora. Still standing columns.*

52. Agora. Portico of Tiberius. West and northwest flanks.

the Italian mission of 1937 that began investigations of its north wing, discovered some of its magnificent friezes and dedicatory inscription honouring the emperor Tiberius (14-37 A.D.) and suggested that it formed part of an agora. The current excavations resumed work along the north wing in the last few years and restored a great number of columns there as well as at its west end where the portico is adjacent to the Baths of Hadrian and at its southeast corner where it abuts the so-called Agora Gate. An impressive series of frieze blocks decorated with handsome masks, individualised or divine faces, joined with garlands, was also recorded in these excavations. Their remarkable variety and execution bear witness to the talents of the local artists and architects.

Preliminary analysis of the architectural features of the portico, such as the capitals and friezes, indicates that the north colonnade was essentially completed in the first half of the first century, but its western end betrayed restoration in the second century, probably after damage caused by an earthquake. On the other hand, the partly uncovered and tentatively reerected columns of the south long side of the portico, are clearly of later vintage, probably from the fifth or sixth century. Two explanations may be suggested for this: either this wing was never completed in the first century *or* it was so badly damaged in the later fourth century earthquakes that it was drastically reworked thereafter, as the flooding problems affecting the agora were being dealt with.

These problems are clearly evident in the monumental structure closing the eastern end of the Portico of Tiberius, the so-called Agora Gate. Built in the middle of the second cen-

53. *Dedicatory architrave inscription of Portico of Tiberius.*

54. *North flank of Portico of Tiberius, with frieze blocks in front.*

55. Female head. From frieze of Portico of Tiberius.

56. Female head. Fom frieze of Portico of Tiberius.

tury and shortly thereafter, this impressive gateway featured an aediculated façade (i.e. with columnar niches) in two stories on the agora side and included two units with barrel-vaulted tunnels projecting like towers at either extremity which joined the colonnades of the portico. Though much destroyed by the seventh century earthquake, the Agora Gate apparently withstood the earlier fourth century ones. However, in the attempts to control the invading ground waters flooding the agora, it was transformed into a *nymphaeum*, or fountainhouse. A pool, or catch-basin, was built in front of it and a terracotta water-pipe system was inserted into its façade in order to permit an orderly channeling of the waters into the catch-basin. Epigraphical evidence, in the form of epigrams carved on the face above the pool, points to a fifth century date for that transformation. Much

57. *Male head (Zeus). From frieze of Portico of Tiberius.*

58. South side of Portico of Tiberius (fifth century) with south "tower" of Agora Gate.

59. Agora Gate and its fifth century catch-basin (nymphaeum).

60. *Restoration drawing of original west façade of Agora Gate (Dinu Theodorescu).*

61. *Amazonomachy panel reused on catch-basin wall of Agora Gate.*

62. *Gigantomachy panel* **(Dioskouroi)** *found near catch-basin of Agora Gate.*

63. *Centauromachy panel. Found near catch-basin of Agora Gate.*

64. *Baths of Hadrian. General view.*

65. *Lifesize* **togatus** *statue. From Agora Gate façade.*
Mid-second century.

statuary that decorated the Agora Gate's niches and many unusual relief panels reused in the masonry of the catch-basin were recovered in the excavations. Among the reliefs are scenes of combats between Centaurs and Lapiths, Gods and Giants, and Amazons and Greeks (Centauromachy, Gigantomachy and Amazonomachy).

The Baths of Hadrian

acing the Agora Gate, at the west end of the Portico of Tiberius, over 200 or so meters distant rise the impressive remains of the Baths of Hadrian. This thermal establishment consisted of an approximately symmetrical grouping of two large galleries on either side of a huge central hall, probably the *calidarium*, and included complicated underground service corridors, furnace rooms and water-channels. The core of the structure was built out of a light sandstone, which was revetted with marble plaques. Various functions, such as *tepidarium, sudatorium apodyterium* and *frigidarium* may be assigned to these galleries.

The Baths of Hadrian were the scene of the principal activities of the French amateur-archaeologist, Paul Gaudin in 1904. Its forecourt, (*palaestra?*) yielded a huge number of architectural fragments, especially beautifully carved large pilasters of the "peopled scrolls" type, featuring figures of Eros, birds and other animals intertwined in scrolls of acanthus leaves that adorned the façade of the baths, and a stunning series of colossal heads, featuring Medusa, Herakles, Perseus, the Minotaur and others in the form of large consoles that decorated the en-

tablatures of the *palaestra* itself. Many unusual full-length statues were discovered in the west portico of the agora. Most of these finds were eventually transported to Istanbul, where they can still be seen in the Archaeological Museum.

Not far from the Hadrianic Baths, near the southwestern corner of the Portico of Tiberius, preliminary investigations brought to light part of a large basilica, an administrative and official building of importance. Its original construction was probably in the late first century, but archaeological evidence indicates that its function assumed greater significance in the second half of the third century. This must be connected with Aphrodisias' increased role as administrative centre and eventually metropolis of the province of Caria after the 250's. Two significant discoveries support such a theory. Many inscribed panels bearing the Latin text of the

66. *"Peopled scrolls" pillar fragment **in situ** in Baths of Hadrian.*

67. *Colossal console head of Herakles, found in 1904 by P. Gaudin in Baths of Hadrian (now in the İstanbul Archaeological Museums).*

68. *Colossal console head of Medusa. Baths of Hadrian.*

69. *Large basilica. General view.*

70. *Panel inscribed with Edict of Prices of Diocletian. (301 A.D.).*

emperor Diocletian's Edict of Maxımum Prices of 301, as well as that of another heretofore unknown companion decree dealing with currency reform were found in or near the entrance of the basilica where they were probably displayed. A number of interesting relief panels, very likely parts of the balustrade for the upper intercolumniations of the building's east aisle were also discovered close to the surface. Several figures shown on these panels were duly identified by inscriptions and included Ninos and Semiramis, naturally portrayed like Roman figures, as well as Gordios, Pegasos, Bellerophon and Apollo. These panels obviously echoed the mythical foundation legends of Aphrodisias alluded to in Stephanus of Byzantium's use of the name Ninoe for the Carian city. The presence of Gordios, on the other hand, the mythical king of Phrygia, may well be associated with Aphrodisias' earlier role as capital of a joint province of Caria and Phrygia.

71. *Balustrade relief showing Ninos officiating at an altar topped by an eagle. From large basilica.*

72. Balustrade relief showing Semiramis and Gordios. From large basilica.

The Sebasteion

Among the most unusual and significant archaeological discoveries made
in recent years not only at Aphrodisias
but also at any classical site, the remarkable
building dedicated to the Imperial cult known
as the *Sebasteion* ranks unquestionably high.
This complex (named after *Sebastos*, Greek
equivalent of the Latin Augustus) was found
fortuitously in 1979 under the expropriated
cottages of Geyre and proved to be a sanctuary
devoted to the cult of the deified emperor
Augustus (alias *Sebastos*), his Julio-Claudian
successors as well as to the goddess Aphrodite
(Venus), from whom the dynasty claimed descent. Located in the southwestern part of the
city, east of the agora, the *Sebasteion*, when
fully revealed, did not show any alignment
with the agora or any structure. It was oriented

east-west and consisted of two long (ca. 80 m.)
parallel porticoes of half columns facing one
another and separated by a paved processional
way (ca. 14 m. wide). At the west, the porticoes were joined in a gateway, or *propylon*,
giving access to a street (the same one that
passed before the *Tetrapylon*). At the opposite
end, a flight of steps, added later in Byzantine times, led to a platform on which stood
the temple, dominating the whole complex.
Although not entirely similar, both porticoes
presented façades not unlike a stage front.
They consisted of three superimposed storeys
of half columns. The lowest order was Doric
topped by less tall Ionic, then still smaller Corinthian half columns.

An unusual number of large relief and
decorative panels were discovered inside and
outside the porticoes, and were clearly meant
to be inserted in the intercolumniations of the

73. *Sebasteion*. General view looking west.

74. Plan of *Sebasteion*.

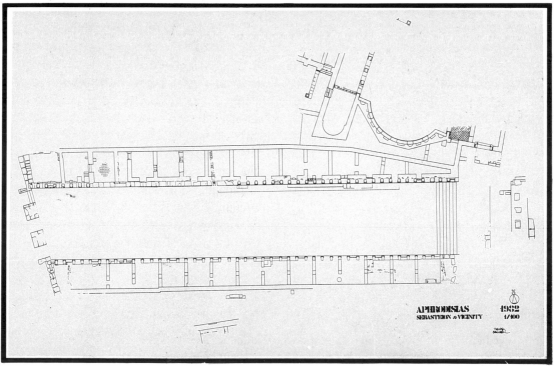

75. *Restoration drawing of façade of south portico of* **Sebasteion** *(F. Hueber, U. Outschar).*

75A Restoration drawing of the Sebasteion and its **propylon** *looking east (F. Biller, G. Kaynak).*

upper two storeys. In the south portico, the second storey featured reliefs that portrayed mythological scenes such as the birth of Eros, the Three Graces, Apollo at Delphi, Meleager, Achilles and Penthesilea, Nyssa and the infant Dionysos, to name only a few. The upper intercolumniations, on the other hand, were fitted with reliefs showing imperial figures among which Augustus, Germanicus, Lucius and Gaius Caesar, Claudius and Agrippina are recognisable, and mythological subjects, such as the liberation of Prometheus, Aeneas fleeing Troy, and others. The most interesting reliefs of this last group included one showing Claudius overwhelming a symbolic representation of Britannia and another Nero seizing a similarly allegorical figure of Armenia, all duly identified by inscriptions on separate bases.

Unfortunately, the north portico was severely hit by the fourth century earthquakes and even more damaged by the seventh century one. As a result, many of the reliefs decorating its intercolumniations were carted away and are missing. Nevertheless, several were found and suggest that personifications of various peoples conquered by Augustus were shown on the panels, and stood on separate *trompe l'oeil* bases decorated with garlanded masks of satyrs, or Pan, and with identifying inscriptions of the peoples involved, e.g. the Judaeans, the Bessi, the Dacians, the Egyptians, the Arabs, etc... The top storey appears to have featured representations of cosmic figures. However, only two of these showing Okeanos and Hemera were found. One well-preserved relief suitably concealed inside the portico and portraying the young Nero in military garb being crowned by his mother Agrippina, was also recovered.

76. *Sebasteion*. Early in the course of excavations.

77. *Sebasteion*. South portico. Three Graces.

78. *Sebasteion*. South portico. Achilles and Penthesilea.

79. *Sebasteion*. *South portico. Meleager (?).*

80. *Sebasteion.South portico. Aeneas fleeing Troy with father and son.*

Epigraphical evidence indicates that the porticoes were dedicated by two different families under the reigns of Claudius and Nero. The *propylon*, whose façade was aediculated, (that is with columnar niches) in two storeys, was offered by the same family that built the north portico and adorned with abundant portrait statuary of the Julio-Claudian family. Unfortunately, only fragments and inscribed bases of these were recovered.

Of the temple itself at the opposite end, only traces of its *crepis* and stylobate as well as architectural elements such as column drums, architrave blocks and Corinthian capitals were found. Later Byzantine and Turkish houses built in this location apparently caused much damage to its remains.

The *Sebasteion* was naturally affected by the fourth century earthquakes, as already

noted, and its subsequent inundations. A complicated series of drainage pipes and water channels was organised near and around the temple and along the processional way in order to evacuate the threatening waters. The *propylon* was also fitted with terracotta pipes and the level of the street passing before it had to be considerably raised. Between the fifth and the seventh century, the complex may have been disaffected or only occasionally used as a market area. Its complete collapse was caused by the seventh century earthquake. Many of its architectural components and sculptured panels of the north portico were scattered and reused in various contexts. Some were incorporated in the fortification wall blocking the theatre stage building when the Acropolis was transformed into a citadel. Others were dragged even further away and fitted into the city walls.

81. *Sebasteion*. South portico. Birth of Eros.

82. *Sebasteion. South portico. Augustus ruling the earth and the seas.*

83. **Sebasteion.** South portico. Liberation of Prometheus by Herakles.

84. **Sebasteion**. *South portico. Claudius overwhelming Britannia (Britain).*

85. **Sebasteion**. *South portico. Claudius and Agrippina.*

86. *Sebasteion*. *South portico. Nero overwhelming Armenia.*

88. *Sebasteion*. *North portico. Base bearing the name of the Bessi.*

87. *Sebasteion*. *North portico. Base bearing the name of the Judaeans.*

89. *Sebasteion*. *North portico. Symbolic relief panel showing personification of the Pirystae.*

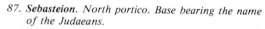

90. **Sebasteion**. *North portico. Symbolic relief of Day (Hemera).*

91. **Sebasteion.** *North portico. Relief panel showing young Nero crowned by his mother Agripina.*

92. **Sebasteion**. *Remain of temple on podium to east.*

Other Areas

Parts of at least six private residences dating to the Roman and early Byzantine periods have been investigated in the past twenty years, more specifically north of the *temenos* of Aphrodite; to the east and south of the *Tetrapylon*; near the northeast city wall; northeast of the *Sebasteion* and by the south city wall.

The plan of the house near the temple of Aphrodite suggests its possible use at one time as a school of philosophy. Most of these residences featured handsome figurative or geometric mosaic pavements in their excavated rooms and yielded unusual artifacts and much pottery. Some appeared to have been abandoned after the seventh century earthquake, and if not, poorly repaired and maintained thereafter.

Other structures partly explored in recent years also include a monastery church complex with a triconch plan and a vast cemetery around it, located to the southwest of the Acropolis, and a small basilica, converted into a church, to the southeast of the Theatre Baths.

Finally, the presence of a sizable Jewish community and the existence of a synagogue at Aphrodisias have been clearly indicated by a series of grafitti in the odeon, the theatre and the *Sebasteion* and an inscribed pillar, found accidentally. The text of this last discovery lists the names of Jews as well as sympathizers, often including their profession. Some of the non-Jews are described as *theosebeis* or god-fearing, and were sympathetic towards Judaism, participating in some rituals, without actually becoming proselytes. Such groups known from the Acts of the Apostles and other sources have been the subject of much discussion and scholarly controversy.

93. *General view of "school of philosophy" residence.*

94. *Early Byzantine house complex to the northeast.*   95. *House complex near the* **Sebasteion.**

96. *"Martyrion" or monastery church.*

97. *Small basilica. South of the site.*

98. *Pillar with inscription (from synagogue ?)*
referring to the Jewish population of Aphrodisias.

The Necropolis

*L*ike all ancient cities, Aphrodisias counted a vast necropolis zone outside its habitation area. This stretched out in all directions beyond the circuit of the fourth century fortifications. Only a very limited number of these tombs has been so far explored. The sarcophagi that decorate the grounds of the museum were collected from various locations outside the city or from village houses where they had been dragged for various reuses.

Aphrodisian sculptors produced many types of sarcophagi. The most frequently encounterred ones were the garland and the columnar variety. At times the former was roughly carved and used unfinished. Several specimens of them have been found and can be seen in the museum gardens and various parts of the site.

99. *Sarcophagus. From west necropolis.*

100. *Garland sarcophagus. From west necropolis.*

101. *Unfinished, fragmentary statue of Hermes.*

The School of Aphrodisias

*T*he results of the last nearly thirty years
of work at Aphrodisias described in the
preceding brief discussions of its chief
monuments have clearly been unusually rich,
varied as well as most significant. No
discoveries, however, have been as stunning
and revealing as the sculpture and marble-
carving activities of the Aphrodisian artists.
The notion of a school of sculpture at
Aphrodisias, first advanced as mentioned
earlier by Maria F. Squarciapino, is now more
valid than ever. Many new sculptors'
signatures can now be added to those collected
by her. Others, already known, have been
given additional dimension to their work
through new discoveries. The presence of the
excellent marble quarries and their proximity
to the city unquestionably played a crucial role

102. *Trial or exercise piece of a front foot.*

103. *Sculptor's signature. Apollonios Aster.*

in the development of sculpture at Aphrodisias. The extraordinary amount of statuary and fragments thereof found during past as well as current excavations is truly unprecedented, and the discovery of dozens of trial or unfinished pieces prove, if any doubt remained, the existence of a true school. Its longevity, stretching over six centuries, from the first century B.C. to the end of the fifth century A.D. is rare indeed, if not unique, and permits a solid assessment of the originality and the contribution of the Aphrodisian artists to Graeco-Roman sculpture.

If the precise origins of this school are not known (some artists could have come from Pergamon in the late second cent. B.C.), the quality of the available marble must have been a great source of attraction. The handsome sculpture created out of this first-class material rapidly earned the Aphrodisians a reputation

104. Sculptor's signature. Alexander, son of Zenon.

105. Marble quarries. East of the city.

106. *Group of portrait heads found in recent excavations.*

107. *Bearded male portrait head. Fifth century.*

that grew from a local to a Mediterranean-wide level and was undoubtedly enhanced by political events, imperial patronage, and essentially peaceful and prosperous conditions. As clearly evident in their creations displayed in the museum (or elsewhere), the Aphrodisian sculptors were the direct descendants of Hellenistic art. They proved themselves virtuosi of marble-carving and asserted their talents by producing statuary blending earlier sources of inspiration with styles and techniques of their own times. There can be no doubt that they have now earned a place of honour in the history of ancient art and sculpture.

ADDENDUM

Continued excavations in 1988 and 1989 have recently revealed a new feature in the layout of the Portico of Tiberius which may alter our views on this part of the agora. A huge basin or pool, ca. 175 m. long, 25 m. wide and almost 1 m. deep and terminating in a semicircle at both east and west extremity seemes to occupy the central area of the portico. Its outer rim consisted of blocks carved like theatre seats, echoing similar features on the stylobate blocks of at least the north and west colonnades. Furthermore, a well-built water channel proved to separate this outer rim from the interior one. At the present stage, it is safe to assume that this "pool" fulfilled both practical and aesthetic purposes. The seat arrangement of the outer rim and of its vis-a-vis on the stylobate of the colonnades north and west imply the seating of spectators. The Portico of Tiberius would then be a gymnasium or a palestra with the area between the colonnade and the pool intended for athletic exercises and contests. The immediate proximity of the Baths of Hadrian, which not only required much water for its needs and services, but also lacked a suitable palestra usual in Roman thermal establishments could explain the presence of the pool. Future excavations will undoubted shed additional light on this unusual and rare feature.

GUIDE TO THE APHRODISIAS MUSEUM

KENAN T. ERİM
with Nathalie de Chaisemartin

108. General view of the Aphrodisias Museum.

Introduction

The Aphrodisias Museum represents the culmination of a project that was conceived already in 1961 with the start of the recent excavations. Indeed, the practice of removing most, if not all, discoveries from their original site, or their vicinity, needed reconsideration. Even if mandatory or useful, this prevented the visitor from appreciating fully the archaeological remains that he viewed. At Aphrodisias, it was considered even more crucial to keep all finds *in situ* and eventually exhibit them there since so much of the recovered material, and above all the sculpture, had been created or fashioned in or near the city *and* adorned its public and private buildings. Prior to the recent excavations, almost all major discoveries had either been taken to the Archaeological Museums of Istanbul or dispersed (Paul Gaudin excavations of 1904-5) or to Izmir (G. Jacopi excavations of 1937). Consequently, from 1961 on, with the authorisation of the General Directorate of Antiquities and Museums, the archaeological material recovered from our investigations was kept in the excavation house stores and safes and in a large storage depot located in the old village of Geyre, close to the spot where the museum was eventually to be built.

At first several alternatives were considered for displaying our new finds. The possibility of converting the Baths of Hadrian into a museum (as had been done with the thermal establishment at Side) was entertained. However, this idea was soon abandoned because of a number of practical problems such as the solidity of the remaining building and the inevitable need for adequate storage facilities. It was, therefore, decided that the most suitable place to plan a building was near one of the main accesses to the site, not far from the main village square of old Geyre. Indeed, as excavations and expropriations progressed, villagers gradually moved a couple of kilometers to the west, to new Geyre.

Several preliminary plans for the museum complex were prepared by expedition architects, but eventually, the final ones were drawn up by Mrs. Erten Altaban, who was then working for the General Directorate of Antiquities and Museums, as the Turkish authorities decided to provide most of the funds. However, a substantial grant from the National Geographic Society considerably accelerated the construction work. Preparations of the exhibits were also helped through other grants, including one from the National Endowment for the Humanities, Washington, D.C. (1976). Turyağ, of Izmir, also allocated funds for completing some of the museum installations.

Construction was started in the winter of 1971-2 and completed in the autumn of 1977. The sculpture items to be exhibited were then gradually moved into the finished halls and necessary restorations undertaken by Mr. Reha Arıcan, then with the Department of Restoration of the Istanbul Archaeological Museums, assisted by Mr. Muhittin Uysal (of the same department). Mr. Özgen Acar, then Director of the Aktur Village Construction, near Bodrum, and Mr. Altan Türe, first Director of the Museum, proved most helpful with the landscaping of the museum gardens and surrounding area. The museum was inaugurated officially on July 21, 1979 by the Hon. Münir Güney, Governor of the Province of Aydın.

The main purposes of the Aphrodisias Museum are to present to the visitor not only samples of all the rich remains unearthed from the archaeological site, but above all to stress the excellence and wide range of sculpture that was produced in Aphrodisian workshops during Roman and Early Byzantine times. Interested persons and specialists can then

109. Bust of emperor Trajan (98-117).

become aware through the high quality of the material on display as well as its abundance that Aphrodisias was undoubtedly one of the main centres of sculpture in Asia Minor *and* the Roman Mediterranean. This was clearly spurred by the presence of white and blue-grey marble quarried on the slopes of the Baba Dağ range to the northeast of the site that provided an excellent material for the Aphrodisian ateliers.Between the first century B.C. and the end of the fifth century A.D., the Aphrodisian sculptors proved themselves virtuosi with their chisels, used techniques that were very sophisticated for their time and enabled them to work with both precision and speed. They executed some remarkable statuary in the Classical Greek and Hellenistic styles, but also produced a series of highly original sculpture and decorative reliefs designed to embellish both private and public buildings. Indeed, if their creations freely echo Greek or Hellenistic prototypes, they also reveal a complex approach that combines a tendency to idealise (as in the portrayal of divine physiognomies) with an emphasis on realism and ornamentation, (evident in the details of bodies). This is frequently associated with a definite mannerism and even baroque style that manifest themselves in the polish of skin and the way in which eyes, hands and drapery are often rendered. Such a composite approach can be detected in sculptures that vary greatly in quality and range from statues of divinities to portraits of individuals, whether well-known philosophers, priests of Aphrodite, members of the imperial family or high officials.

The Aphrodisians were also expert in handling in a most original way architectural decoration and certain elements used in the adornment of buildings, such as pillars featuring scrolls of acanthus with interspersed human and animal figures ("peopled scrolls"), revetment capitals, tondo busts, or relief panels depicting mythological themes. It is, therefore, not surprising that the Aphrodisian workshops exported finished or semifinished products that were in demand abroad, and even its skilled craftsmen who worked in Rome and elsewhere around the Mediterranean, in North Africa, for example, where they may heve been involved with the decoration of the Forum of Septimius Severus at Leptis Magna, in Libya. Over thirty sculptors' signatures, accompanied by the adjective *Aphrodisieus* ("from Aphrodisias") can be recorded from various parts of the Empire, while many new as well as already known names were found on sculpture or fragments unearthed in excavations since 1961.

The halls of the Aphrodisias Museum are arranged around a central courtyard. Starting on the right of the entrance hall the museum should be visited in an anticlockwise direction. Artifacts are arranged thematically, rather than chronologically, so that each room is devoted to one aspect of Aphrodisian sculpture: busts, decorative sculpture, and religious sculpture. Ceramics and other objects can be seen in the Display Case Gallery*.

1. (E. 65.224 and 66.813 M. 79.10.156). This bust, which was found in the Baths of Hadrian, is based on a well-known portrait-type of the emperor Trajan. It may either represent the emperor himself or an individual portrayed in the emperor's likeness.

2. (E. 61.81 M. 79.10.157) Facing this bust is a statue of a male figure wearing the Greek outer garment, or *himation*. Found to the east of the Odeon. The shape of the shoes and the bundles of documents behind his left leg indicate that he was a local notable of the Roman period.

* The letters E and M given for each exhibit item refers respectively to excavation and museum inventory numbers.

The Imperial Hall

3. (E. 72.438 M. 79.10.158) Headless statue of a young man wearing the *himation*. From the vicinity of the Odeon.

4. (E. 67.282 to 285, 71.477 M. 79.10.159) Statue of the emperor Domitian, (81 - 96 A.D.) who, after his death, was given the penalty of the *damnatio memoriae* (condemnation of memory), which decreed the suppression of all statues and inscriptions in his honour. The statue, found in pieces in the orchestra of the theatre, is therefore, a rare example: its inscription shows that it was erected at the request of the people and through the good offices of a local notable, Diogenes, son of Eukleos. It dates from the early years of the emperor's reign (84 A.D.).

5. (E. 70.742 M. 79.10.160) Over-lifesize female statue, also found in the theatre. It probably represents an empress, draped in a veil according to the model of *Pudicitia* (personification of chastity or modesty in women), and with her face hidden behind her veil.

6. (E. 73.240 M. 79.10.161) Portrait head of the empress Livia, wife of Augustus, found north of the theatre stage. The knot of hair which covered the forehead, was executed separately and has disappeared.

7. (E. 70.481 M. 70.10.162) Portrait head of an elderly man with a veil; his thin neck is lined, with folds of skin emphasized. It can be identified as a posthumous portrait of Julius Caesar, resembling that on his coins for 44 B.C., year of his assassination (see fig. 9).

8. (E. 72.1 M. 79.10.163) Female statue discovered on the foundations of the museum. It is a representation of the Hellenistic type known as the *Grande Herculanaise* whose drapery forms a triangle across her left breast and arm, a type which was often used for funerary and honorific statues of Roman

110. Full portrait statue and inscribed base of the emperor Domitian (81-96). From the Theatre.

111. "Pudicitia" type female statue. From the Theatre.

matrons. The bunch of poppies and ears-of-corn which she holds in her left hand indicates that she was initiated into the mysteries of Demeter.

9. (E. 68.341A and 70.496 M. 79.10.164) Large female statue wearing a *peplos*, work of the sculptor Apollonios. Originally in the Theatre. The head, crowned with a diadem, is probably an idealised portrait of the empress Sabina, Hadrian's wife. Her pose is similar to that of the bronze "dancers" from Herculaneum. These *peplos*-clad statues are based on fifth-century B.C. Greek models (the style known as "severe") and were popular during the reign of Hadrian (second cent. A.D.).

10. (E. 72.439 M. 79.10.165) In the centre of the room stands a large headless statue of an emperor (?) in military dress. He is wearing a breastplate decorated with griffins - the symbols of the forces of the good - facing each other, the commander's belt (*cingulum*) and the large cloak worn by officers (*paludamentum*). A ceremonial helmet, with the crest supported by a sphinx, is placed at his feet and bears the signature of the sculptor, Apollonios Aster, son of Chrysippus (see also fig. 103).

11. (E. 66.212 M. 79.10.166) Female portrait, from the Julio-Claudian Period (first half of the first cent. A.D.). Found in the Theatre.

12. (E. 63.600 M. 79.10.167) Portrait head of a young boy dating from the Julio-Claudian period. Discovered in the Baths of Hadrian.

13. (E. 72.440 M. 79.10.168) Large headless male statue wearing a tunic and *himation*: his shoes and the ring on his left hand show that he was either a prince or a notable of the city during the Roman period.

14. (E. 72.441 M. 79.10.169) Large male torso, found to the east of the Odeon. It is nude with a cloak draped over his left shoulder and covering his thighs. This torso is probably from the statue of an emperor depicted as a hero or a divinity.

15. (E. 72.203 M. 79.10.170) Portrait head of a young prince of the Constantinian dynasty. Found near the Theatre. It was recarved from a previous head which must have belonged to the statue wearing a *toga* (no. 16). The treatment of the face is sensitive and realistic. it was adorned with a crown of cabochons, but only empty sockets for these remain.

16. (E. 72.131 M. 79.10.171) Under life-size, headless statue of an adolescent. It is an honorific statue, dressed in the *toga* and buskins of a senator. Executed with delicacy, this statue dates from the Julio-Claudian period. The head described above at no.15 probably belonged to this figure.

112. Colossal statue of emperor (?) in military dress, signed by Apollonios Aster, son of Chrysippus.

113. Head reworked as portrait of a Constantinian prince.

Entrance to the Corridor of Zoilos

17. (E. 68.341 M. 79.10.172) Female portrait head, dating from the Julio-Claudian period.

18. (E. 72.234 M. 79.10.173) Female portrait head. The base of a statue dedicated to the Elder Agrippina (found together with this head in the *tetrastoon* behind the stage wall) suggests that it may represent this princess, wife of Germanicus and mother of the emperor Caligula. If so, it is a highly idealised posthumous portrait (37-41 A.D.).

Corridor of Zoilos

19. (E. 61.2, 43, 60, 61, 62, 63, 70.630 M. 79.10.174) The Zoilos Frieze. This series

of panels belonged to an honorific monument commemorating Zoilos, a freedman of Octavian, who hailed from Aphrodisias and was benefactor of his native city during the second half of the first century B.C.. He was responsible, in particular, for the construction of the theatre stage. These panels were found to the northwest of the city, behind the museum. It is not yet possible to establish the exact location and shape of the edifice which they once decorated.

1st Panel: On the left, a herm (rectangular pillar terminating in a bust) close to a hanging wreath marks the spot where the scene takes place, probably a public square or gymnasium in front of a sanctuary. The personification of the People, Demos, who is identified by an inscription, is moving right towards Zoilos. He is wearing a *himation* and carrying a sceptre with a carved pommel which he is pointing at the wreaths hanging on the wall in the background.

2nd Panel: Zoilos is standing opposite Demos, his right arm stretched out towards him. He is dressed like a traveller, and wears a round hat (*petasus*), and a short cloak (*chlamys*) over a wide-sleeved tunic.

3rd Panel: A female figure, the symbol of the City (Polis), is holding a crown over Zoilos' head. Turned three-quarters to the right, the goddess is wearing a *peplos* and a veil whose folds are billowing in the wind. Her diadem is surmounted by a mural crown, the traditional attribute of allegorical figures of cities.

4th Panel: Under two hanging crowns, Zoilos is shown in the stance of a Roman orator, wearing a *toga* wrapped tightly around his body (*toga adstricta*) that was fashionable towards the end of the Roman Republic. On the right, a standing female figure, shown from the front, raises her right arm over Zoilos' head as as sign of protection, or may

114. General view of Zoilos reliefs.

be holding a now missing crown (?). Wearing only a simple mantle which covers her left shoulder and is draped over her thighs, and holding a cornucopia, this goddess is identified as Timé (Honour), by an inscription.

5th Panel: Female figure turned three-quarters towards the right, with her left knee forward, holding a shield decorated with the head of a Gorgon. It is Andreia, the personification of Valour (*Virtus*). Her pose is not unlike that of figures of Victory who are often shown inscribing the exploits of victors on a shield.

6th Panel: An old man is shown in profile, on the right, seated on a rock. He is bearded and is wearing a long-sleeved tunic and cloak which covers his head. He is pressing his right hand against his temple, in a pose characteristic of the Roman god of Time, Saturn. Here, the Greek name Aion, which means Eternity is inscribed above.

7th Panel: A woman wearing a helmet is seated facing left; she is dressed in a tunic revealing her right shoulder and breast. She is leaning against a votive shield, which is attached to a plinth and is holding a spear in her right hand. Although no inscription is preserved, she is recognisable as the goddess Roma armed and dressed like an Amazon.

This partly preserved group of reliefs testifies to the great skill which the Aphrodisian sculptors were already demonstrating by the second half of the first century B.C., and glorify Zoilos as well as the links between Aphrodisias and Rome.

115. *Zoilos being crowned by Polis.*

116. *Head of Polis.*

Hall of Melpomene

Several portraits datable from the second to the fifth centuries A.D. are displayed in this hall, as well as a group of statues which were originally part of the theatre decoration.

On the right as one enters:

20. (E. 75.206 M. 79.10.175) This portrait head, found in the south wall of the city, belonged to the figure of a deceased woman, lying on a *kline* (funerary bed) sarcophagus and leaning on her left elbow, as suggested by the remains of the fingers of her left hand resting on her jawbone. The hairstyle indicates a date in the reigns of Severan emperors (early third cent. A.D.).

Along the right wall stand statues of Aphrodisian notables which date from the late Roman period (late fourth-fifth century).

21. (E. 75.248 M. 79.10.176) The first, found to the west of the Portico of Tiberius, is of an emperor or prince who is holding up the handkerchief (*mappa*) which was thrown into the arena as a signal for the start of the games; in his left hand, he holds a sceptre. Some details - such as the way in which the *toga* is draped, with the narrow-sleeved tunic worn underneath, and the laced-up gaiters- recall the statue of Valentinian II also found nearby in 1904 now in the Istanbul Archaeological Museum and suggest a date towards the end of the fourth century.

22. (E. 64.428 M. 79.10.177) *Toga*-clad magistrate. Fifth cent. A.D..

23. (E. 67.82 M. 79.10.178) Portrait head of an older man whose expression recalls fifth-century male portrait types.

24. (E. 65.199 M. 79.10.179) Headless portrait statue of a magistrate called Oikoumenios. His name is known from the inscribed base on which the statue stood, behind the stage of the odcon. He is wearing the long Byzantine-style mantle (*chlamys*) and is holding a parchment scroll, the insignia of his office (fifth cent. A.D.).

25. (E. 66.516, 517, 518 M. 79.10.180) Statue of a magistrate, also wearing a *chlamys*, accompanied by two children (the one to the right has almost completely disappeared). The remaining child is dressed, like his father, in a tunic, but is also draped in a mantle (*himmation*) and wears a medallion (*bulla*) around his neck (fifth cent. A.D.).

At the far end of the room:

26. (E. 72.49. M. 79.10.181) Full-scale statue of Flavius Palmatus, governor of the Roman province of Asia towards the end of the fifth century A.D. Its inscribed base was found together with the figure in the *tetratsoon* behind the theatre stage. The official is holding a handkerchief (*mappa*) and carries a sceptre in his left hand. The *toga*, with its stiff pleats, forms a sort of scarf which is tightly wrapped around his chest and left shoulder. His thick, curly hair, his partly shaven beard and his stern expression recall official Byzantine portraits from the second half of the fifth century.

27. (E. 69.210 M. 79.10.182) Male portrait head found near the Baths of Hadrian, in the west wing of the Portico of Tiberius. It is remarkable for its realistic expression and should be dated to the Constantinian period.

28. (E. 69.431 M. 79.10.183) This male portrait, found in the southwestern portion of the Portico of Tiberius, recalls the portrait of Flavius Palmatus in the stylisation of its

117. *Full-length portrait statue of Flavius Palmatus, "vicar" of Asia. Later fifth century.*

118. Melpomene. Muse of Tragedy. From the Theatre.

austere and emaciated face framed by a fringe of curly hair. Second quarter of the fifth century A.D.

On the left of the room are three colossal statues which belonged to the decoration of the theatre stage, where they were probably placed in a niche. Indeed, their backs have been partially hollowed out to make them lighter.

29. (E. 70.473 M. 79.10.184) (E. 70.628 M. 79.10.186). These two symmetrical statues of Melpomene, Muse of Tragedy, are depicted wearing *peploi* and holding tragic masks with long curly wigs. They are wearing theatrical high-heeled shoes (*cothurni*). The mouth of the figure with its head preserved is open as though she were declaiming.

30. (E. 70.474 M. 79.10.185) This figure shows Apollo as a musician probably playing a cithara: he is wearing a long robe and flowing mantle. These three statues may date from the reign of Tiberius (early first cent. A.D.).

31. (E. 71.151 M. 79.10.187) Head of Apollo from the Theatre. His expression of ecstasy (eyes raised towards the sky) and his stylised hair are reminiscent of a type found in the Antonine period (later second cent. A.D.).

Going back towards the entrance of the hall the following items can be seen:

32. (E. 62.489, 63.72, 68.484 M. 79.10.188) Statue of a magistrate wearing a *toga*, with a battered head showing a thick fringe of tight curls. Found in the Odeon (fifth cent. A.D.).

33. (E. 63.533 M. 79.10.189) Expressive portrait head of a young woman, found near the north-east wall of the city. Her hairstyle suggests a date in the fourth century A.D.

At the junction of the Hall of Melpomene and the Odeon Hall, stand two statues of boxers or pugilists that face one another. Both were found on the stage of the theatre.

119. Head of Apollo. Later second century.

120. Full-length statue of a boxer or pugilist. ca. 230.

34. (E. 70.508-511, 71.374 M. 79.10.190) Statue of boxer, signed on the front of its plinth by the Aphrodisian sculptor Polyneikes. This artist is also known from a signature found in Rome.

35. (E. 67.287, 288, 443, 68.397, 71.338 M. 79.10.191) Matching piece of no.34.

These two figures represent middle-aged athletes, whose faces and ears are scarred from the blows which they have received in their professional lives. Their heads are shaven, except for a star-shaped tuft of hair on top. Their anatomy is depicted in meticulous detail and emphasizes their powerful musculature. Their arms are protected by long boxing arm coverings which are studded and secured by crossed straps. These "gloves" were surely made of leather and trimmed with lead studs and spikes which stuck out at the knuckle (cf. the right hand of no.34). These are clearly portraits datable to the second quarter of the third century A.D.

Odeon Hall

This hall houses several seated statues, mainly of philosophers or poets, a genre in which Aphrodisian workshops often excelled. Unfortunately, the heads of these figures are missing and, therefore, the sitters cannot be identified.

36. (E. 62.451, 452, 486 M. 79.10.192) Colossal standing statue, personification of the People (*Demos*) shown as a man dressed in a tunic and cloak. He is wearing a ring on his middle finger left and must have held a scepter, a scroll or a dish (*patera*) in his right hand. The inscription on its plinth shows that the statue was dedicated to the People by the city council (*boulé*).

37. (E. 62.485 M. 79.10.193) Seated

philosopher (or poet) wearing a tunic and cloak; he probably held a scroll. The head, hands and feet were added separately. The chair with cabriole legs is adorned with a cushion. From the Odeon.

38. (E. 62.491 M. 79.10.194) Philosopher seated on a bench with a cushion. He is wrapped in a mantle that leaves his right torso and arm bare. From the Odeon.

39. (E. 77.77 M. 79.10.195). Elderly philosopher, sitting hunched over and draped in a cloak. He is wearing a ring on the middle finger of his left hand. Found before the Agora Gate catch-basin.

In the corner of the hall:

40. (E. 63.454 M. 79.10.196) Fragmentary statue of Apollo sitting on his mantle spread over a rock. The god is recognisable by the long locks of hair falling on his shoulder and chest.

In front of the pillar in the corridor which runs alongside the Odeon Hall.

41. (E. 62.699 M. 79.10.197) Draped female statue of the *Grande Herculanaise* type often used for funerary and honorific statues of Roman ladies. Part of her mantle covers her head and is draped in a large triangle across her breast towards her left shoulder and arm. Found in the Odeon, this skilfully carved but battered figure is datable to the second century A.D.

42. (E. 65.27 M. 79.10.198) Double-headed herm with the busts of two philosophers, one with thick hair and beard, probably Xenophon, the other bald and bearing a resemblance to Socrates. These herms, were designed to decorate porticoes and gardens in Roman times and often used portrait types of intellectuals renowned for their opposing or

121. Odeon. Seated philosopher or poet.

122. Odeon. Seated philosopher or poet.

pessimism of Epicurus' philosophy of materialism.

46. (E. 65.116, 395 M. 79.10.202) Draped statue of a male figure wearing the *himation*. It originally stood on an inscribed base which identified him as a third century notable called Alexandros Dikaios.

In the middle of the hall:

47. (E. 67.166 M. 79.10.203) Round altar found in the circular tomb (*heroon*) or small sanctuary located behind the Odeon. The top part is hollow and the face of the cylinder is decorated with three Erotes bearing garlands of leaves and fruits.

Near the steps:

complementary ideas and therefore placed back to back.

43. (Discovered in 1956, M. 79.199) Head of an intellectual with a stern expression, and a low forehead: the headband in his hair could suggest a tragic poet (Aeschylus?), but a faint resemblance to Socrates is also evident.

44. (E. 64.144 M. 79.10.200) The type for this portrait was for a long time identified with the Spartan general Pausanias. However, a recent find of an *imago clipeata*, or tondo, portrait bearing an identifying inscription indicates that this head portrayed the fifth-century B.C. lyric poet Pindar. Found in the vicinity of the Odeon.

45. (E. 71.161 M. 79.10.201) Portrait of the philosopher Epicurus. Excellent copy of the third century B.C. original portrait. The long austere-looking face seems to reflect the

48. (E. 63.160 M. 79.10.204) Youthful head of Apollo crowned with laurels. Only its front part is entirely finished. The god is shown in an attitude of ecstasy and his face reflects an expression of "pathos" almost baroque - much favoured by second-century A.D. Aphrodisian artists.

49. (E. 72.50 M. 79.10.205) Male portrait found behind the back of the theatre stage. It was originally a bearded man after the fashion of the emperor Hadrian; in the third century A.D. his hair was recarved to look thinner and his eyes hollowed out into a halfmoon shape. This is a typical instance of how portraits that were no longer in favour, or had not been sold, could be reused or refashioned to suit contemporary taste.

The gallery which runs along the west side of the Melpomene and Odeon Halls displays unfinished sculptures, which are valuable documents on the work and techniques of Aphrodisian sculptors.

123. Partly finished statue of a Constantinian official.

50. (E. 75.207 M. 79.10.206) An unfinished herm, found in the south rampart of the city. Only the face has been completely cut away from the marble slab; marks are visible from the pick and drill used to break up the larger pieces of marble. The head of the herm shows an archaistic Dionysos with a stylised beard. He is wearing a turban-like headdress crowned with fruit and leaves.

51. (E. 69.425, 429, 329 M. 79.10.207) *Toga*-clad statue found to the north of the Odeon. It is under-lifesize: its unfinished head is disproportionately large in relation to the body. The figure, who is holding an inkwell (?) in his left hand, must have had a quill in his right. Found close to a sculpture workshop, it must have been a reject, whose portrait head had barely been outlined. Late Constantinian period.

52. (E. 77.565 M. 79.10.208) Unfinished statue of the sea-god Poseidon, found to the northwest of the Odeon. The figure, who was probably armed with a trident, had a sea dragon (or dolphin?) serving as support. Its sides and back have been only rough-hewn. The left arm was carved separately and attached.

53. (E. 61.84 M. 79.10.209) Statue of Hermes, the messenger god, found in the east necropolis. The figure, wearing a *chlamys* fastened at his shoulder, and carrying the *caduceus* has not been entirely freed from the marble block. Its back remains unfinished (see fig. 101).

54. (E. 63.657 M. 79.10.210) Unfinished high relief showing an athlete at rest holding a discus (?) perhaps inspired by the so-called Diskophoros created by the fifth century B.C. sculptor Polykleitos. The figure is leaning on his elbow against a projection in the stone. It is possible to see some of the drill-holes that outline its curly hair. Its body still reveals grooves from the tooth chisel, generally used

124. Unfinished relief showing a "Diskophoros" type athletic figure.

during the last stage of carving before the polishing process.

55. (E. 64.4. M. 79.10.211) Idealised female head which betrays various stages of sculptural carving: the face has been worked with the tooth chisel, the hair with the point, the top of the head has been rough-hewn , while the back of the head remains unfinished.

56. (E. 76.35 M. 79.10.212) Unfinished head of an adolescent found near the Theatre Baths. It is in the pre-polishing stage, although the process was started. The hairstyle suggests a date in the Julio-Claudian period.

57. (E. 69.426 M. 79.10.213) Lower body of a drunken satyr lying on a rock. Found north of the Odeon. The figure is lying on a panther's skin and is holding a drinking vessel (*rhyton*) in its left hand in the direction of a crawling serpent. The plinth is unfinished and the satyr's body unpolished. This type of sculpture, known from several copies (for example, the Barberini Faun in Munich), was often used to decorate a fountain or a grotto.

Against the pillar at the corner of the Odeon Hall:

58. (E. 69.70 M. 79.10.214) Statuette of Artemis, goddess of the hunt found to the north of the Odeon. It reproduces the type known as the Versailles Artemis. The front part is cut away from a block which is unworked at the back. The figure has been roughly carved with a flat chisel.

Against the second pillar by the Odeon Hall:

59. (E. 70.524 M. 79.10.215) Low relief found in the theatre depicting a seated oriental warrior, wearing close-fitting breeches, a belted tunic and a cloak. A spear, a sword and an oval shield are shown alongside.

60. (E. 69.185 M. 79.10.216) Statuette of a seated Aphrodite found north of the Odeon. Only the lower part of the figure is preserved. The goddess is sitting, her legs crossed, on a rock covered with a drapery. Only the visible parts at the front of the figure are polished. This suggests that the statuette was used to decorate a niche. It represented Aphrodite arranging or drying her hair.

61. (E. 75.22 M. 79.10.217) Funerary stele of a market supervisor, found in the south city wall. The deceased, whose name has disappeared, is represented in a relief, partly draped bust. Below is an inscription which reveals that the figure held the position of municipal market supervisor.

125. *Seated Aphrodite.*

Display Case Gallery

In the corner niche of the pillar which marks the entrance to the gallery:

62. (E. 66.297, 68.288 M. 79.10.218) High quality, fragmentary head of Athena wearing a helmet decorated with rams' heads.

A row of sculptures is displayed in front of the right window:

63. (E. 73.1 M. 79.10.219) Torso of a young man wearing a *toga,* reused in the backwall of the theatre stage after the seventh century earthquake. The portrait head must have fitted into the neck socket. Turn of the second century A.D.

64. (E. 70.455 M. 79.10.220) Small unfinished male torso, possibly a figure of Hermes carrying the *caduceus*.

126. *General view of display case gallery.*

65. (E. 72.325 M. 79.10.221) Statuette of Asklepios, god of medicine, after the type of the cult-statue of his temple in Rome.The god is leaning on a stick wedged under his right armpit.

66. (E. 67.562 M. 79.10.222) Statuette of Aphrodite found in the northwest back part of the Odeon. It is derived from the famous Aphrodite of Knidos by Praxiteles, but the thin elongated proportions of its torso reflect canons of the late second-century A.D.

67. (E. 70.462 M. 79.10.223) Torso of Dionysos found in the theatre excavations. The god of vegetation and wine is wearing the kidskin (*nebris*).

68. (E. 66.2 M. 79.10.224) Statuette of a headless barbarian prisoner, in violet and white breccia. His arms are bound behind his back. Similar, large polychrome marble statues were used in Rome, in the Forum of the emperor Trajan. This version may have adorned a table or other piece of furniture.

69. (E. 76.10 M. 79.10.225) Statue of a child holding a bird, a type of funerary representation where the bird symbolizes the soul of the dead child.

Display Cases

Against the wall on the left of the entrance, two display cases contain the finds of excavations carried out in the pre- and proto-historic *höyüks* of Aphrodisias, the Acropolis and the mound known as "Pekmez" in the eastern sector of the site.

This part of the collection consists mainly of ceramic finds, vases, pitchers with handles, double-handled tumblers (*depas amphikypellon*), tripod vases, and dishes. A number of small stone idols, often of the violin-shaped variety are also on display. A small vase, a gold necklace and two silver bracelets pertain to an Early Bronze Age pithos burial, found in the "Pekmez" mound.

A smaller case to the left of the room contains a large "Carian" funcrary jar (*dinos*) datable to the Archaic period (seventh century B.C.).

In the middle of the room stand a row of display cases arranged around the gallery from right to left.

One of these displays objects from the Greek and Roman periods. On the top shelf are vases, painted sherds and terracotta figurines of the Archaic period found in the temple and showing a seated goddess probably the Aphrodite of Aphrodisias. A seal (?) which dates from the Roman period portrays the crowned bust of Aphrodite. On the middle shelf are Roman lamps and small marble ex-votos showing body parts healed by the intervention of a divinity of medicine, possibly Asklepios. The bottom shelf displays small bronze objects from the Roman and Byzantine times, the crosspiece of scales, weights, and candlesticks.

On the top shelf of another display case is a collection of Roman glassware some with relief decoration. Many have become irridescent through oxydation from the soil. Below are several small ovoid phials decorated with Christian symbols (*ampullae*), Byzantine lamps, and a collection of glazed plates from the Byzantine and Islamic period, incised with geometric or other designs.

In the small case at the end of the series are a number of objects, some of which are funerary accoutrements of Byzantine tombs. These are arranged around a candelabrum designed to hold a lamp. Here are wooden combs, ivory pins, small ivory precision scales decorated with incisions, and especially jewellery: a small bronze box was found on the Acropolis and contained a necklace and other golden ornaments. There are also several

127. *Small bearded head (late second, early third century).*

bracelets, rings, pendants and earrings, as well as large pearl buttons and beautiful pectoral crosses with incised designs.

The last display case, opposite the door leading to the interior courtyard, contains small-scale creations from Aphrodisian marble workshops. In the centre are several sculptors tools: points, a flat chisel, a double-tooth chisel, and a finely worked bronze gouging rasp.

Heads, idealised figures and small portraits are arranged on the shelves, in particular a bust of Penthesilea (from the group of Penthesilea and Achilles). An unfinished statuette of Apollo wearing a long robe can also be seen, as well as a male torso again from a small replica of the Achilles and Penthesilea group, (a large replica of this composition is on display in the next hall).

128. *Polychrome Europa seated on a bull.*

As already mentioned Aphrodisian sculptors obtained their supplies of marble from the nearby quarries which yielded white as well as blue-veined marble. Their ateliers often specialised in statuettes cut at the intersection of a white and a black vein: a statuette showing Europa, white against her blue bull, and an Eros with blue wings are two interesting examples of this polychromy.

Close to this display case:

70. (E. 44 M. 79.10.226) Torso from a statuette of Herakles, leaning on a stick wedged under his left armpit; inspired by the statue created by the fourth century B.C. sculptor Lysippus .

71. (E. 75.64 M. 79.10.227) and 79. (E. 75. 79 M. 79.10.228) Fragmentary reliefs belong-

129. Sarcophagus fragment showing an Amazonomachy motif (borrowed from the Athena Parthenos' shield decoration).

ing to a sarcophagus showing an Amazonomachy (combat between Greeks and Amazons) inspired by the decoration on the shield of the famous chryselephantine statue of Athena Parthenos by Pheidias, in Athens. These reliefs, found near the south wall of the city, are placed on either side of the stairs leading to the Hall of Penthesilea. On the right, a male figure wearing a tunic and a *chlamys* is stepping up towards the left; below is the helmeted head of an Amazon. On the left, the fragment shows the lower part of an Amazon in a short pleated tunic with a double axe, the favourite weapon of these women warriors, probably being seized by a Greek warrior.

Hall of Penthesilea

This hall contains a variety of sculptures created by Aphrodisian artists, echoing Hellenistic art, or variations of well-known Classical models.

At the bottom of the staircase, to the right along the north wall:

72. (E. 70.502-505 M. 79.10.229) Lifesize replica of the Diskophoros by Polykleitos, which mirrors with remarkable precision its fifth-century B.C. bronze model. The young athlete is standing at rest. He is crowned with the victor's fillet and probably held a discus (?). The back was not finished as the figure was meant to stand in a niche. The eyelashes and locks of hair highlighted with brown paint provide clear proof that ancient statues were partly coloured. This statue testifies to the degree of perfection attained by the Aphrodisians in the first and second centuries A.D. in reproducing models originally created many centuries before.

130. Replica of Polykleitos' Diskophoros.

73. (E. 67.556 M. 79.10.230) Statue (two-third lifesize) showing the young Herakles crowned with oak leaves. Its small head and the elongated proportions of its torso suggest that this may be a replica of one of the statues in the series of the Labours of Herakles executed by the sculptor Lysippus for a sanctuary in Epirus in the fourth century B.C.. The excessive elongation of the torso and legs betrays a tendency often characteristic of Aphrodisian art in the second half of the second century A.D..

In the north-west corner of the hall:

74. (E. 70.492 M. 79.10.231) Corner *akroterion* from the Theatre, consisting of stylised acanthus leaves with rising stalks out. Its edges may have been originally in-

crusted with coloured marble studs. These decorative elements adorned the top of the wall of the stage of the Theatre. First cent. B.C..

75. (E. 67.559 M. 79.10.232) Small-scale replica of a much copied group which showed the god Pan extracting a thorn from the foot of a satyr (*spinario*). Found to the north of the Odeon. The satyr, is clinging to the rock on which he is seated. Pan is portrayed as usual as half-man, half-goat, with horns, big ears and goat's legs. This group also comes from the remains of a workshop behind the Odeon.

76. (E. 67.557, 69.43, 111, 179 M. 79.10. 233)

77. (E. 67.588, 69.128, 183, 184, 575 M. 79.10.234) Two replicas, one two-third lifesize, and the other over-lifesize, of the group of the satyr carrying the child Dionysos and offering him a bunch of grapes (now lost), have been placed side by side. They both come from the northwest end of the back of the Odeon and provide good examples of different scale sculptures of the same subject. A large replica of this group was found in Rome, signed by Flavius Zenon, and belonged to several other statues also signed by Aphrodisian artists, now in the Ny Carlsberg Glyptotek in Copenhagen. The small replica here represents the satyr with elongated proportions and a detailed musculature, which is contrasted with the plump body of the child. The larger replica is a finer specimen. Its back is carefully executed and the satyr's smiling face is highly animated. On the limbs and the sides of his body, veins and tendons are shown in relief, a feature of anatomical representation not uncommon in the work of second-century Aphrodisian artists. The satyr is carrying a hooked shepherd's staff (*pedum*). However, a study of the aforementioned examples discovered in Rome and now in Copenhagen and their signatures suggest that these statues were pro-

131. *Satyr with infant Dionysos (by Fl. Zenon).*

*132. Small version of satyr with infant **Dionysos**.*

133. Achilles and Penthesilea group.

bably executed (or reworked?) in the fourth century A.D. and that Flavius Zenon must therefore be dated to that period.

78. (E. 66.541, 67.10, 31 M 79.10.235) Colossal group of Achilles and Penthesilea which decorated the pool of a *frigidarium* in the Baths of Hadrian. The group illustrates an episode in the Trojan War. During a battle between Amazons and Greeks, the hero Achilles slew Penthesilea, queen of the Amazons, but fell in love with her as she died. The naked warrior, armed with his sword, supports the dying queen, who is wearing a tunic exposing her right breast - and a Phrygian cap (Phrygia was one of the regions of the Anatolian plateau where the Amazons were purported to come from). Penthesilea's wound was painted in red to show the flow of blood.

There are a few other, less complete, replicas of this group among others in the Museo delle Terme in Rome. The composition shows clear similarity with the group of the vanquished Gaul committing suicide after killing his wife (also in the Museo delle Terme, Rome). The original of this belonged, along with the famous dying Gaul in the Capitoline Museum, to a group dedicated by Attalus I, king of Pergamum, to commemorate his victory over the Gauls ca. 230 B.C..

In front of the pillar on the south side of the hall:

79. (E. 63.198 M. 79.10.236) Small torso of Artemis, goddess of the hunt, wearing a light tunic.

80. (E. 67.28-29 M. 79.10.237) Colossal male torso found in the Baths of Hadrian, probably representing a deified emperor in heroic nudity.

81. (E. 75.193 M. 79.10.238) Large head of the emperor Claudius, found to the east end of the Agora. It is a portrait of the deified emperor probably executed after his death (54 A.D.).

82. (E. 67.567 M. 79.10.239) Statue of a child, found in the northwest back of the Odeon. His hairstyle is similar to that of Eros, the god of love: he has a small plait on the crown of his head (*skorpios*) but no wings are visible on his back.

83. (E. 70.499 M. 79.10.240) Nude male torso of the heroic type; the left arm, executed separately, was raised. Found in the Theatre.

84. (E. 74.245 M. 79.10.241) Torso of a winged Victory, found in the courtyard of the Theatre Baths. The goddess is draped in a *peplos* which clings to her body, as she moves against the wind.

Against the double pillar, in the corridor which runs along the Hall of Aphrodite:

85. (E. 70.497 M. 79.10.242) Statuette of a winged Victory (Nike), carrying a palm leaf in the crook of her left arm. Originally decorating the stage of the Theatre.

86. (E. 71.160 M. 79.10.243) Statuette of of a Victory (Nike), also from the theatre stage.

Further along the gallery, near the windows of the courtyard:

87. (E. 64.29 M. 79.10.244) and **88.** (E. 63.620 M. 79.10.245) Two heads, showing the god Apollo, with a knot of hair on the crown of his head (*krobylos*). No 87 seems lost in reverie because of its gaze under heavy eyelids (Apollo was the god of poetical inspiration). No.88 betrays simpler lines and modelling.

Hall of Aphrodite

This hall is essentially devoted to works of sculpture associated with the cult of the goddess of the city, Aphrodite of Aphrodisias. Her large cult-statue stands in the centre of the hall.

On the right, at the bottom of the stairs leading from the Penthesilea Hall:

89. (E. 66.271 M. 79.10.246) Large head of Apollo found in the Baths of Hadrian. It is hollow at the back, and must have been placed fairly high up in the niche of a façade. It clearly shows traces of brown-red paint on the eyebrows and on the hair where it was applied before eventual gilding.

90. (E. 62.447, 487, 63.25 M. 79.10.247) Over-lifesize statue of a priest of Aphrodite. Found in the Odeon. This elderly gentleman wears a double fillet surmounted with medallions or busts which are now lost. He wears a large mantle (*himation*) over his tunic and dates from the Constantinian period. His headdress indicates that he was a priest of Aphrodite, whose bust once decorated the centre of the double fillet.

91. (E. 71.152, 154 M. 79.10.248) Over-lifesize statue of a priest of Aphrodite, found at the centre of the theatre stage. His wrinkled face is executed with the realism characteristic of Roman portraiture. He wears the same dress as the previous priest (no.90). He is also datable to the Constantinian period.

92. (E. 63.57, 64.292, 426 M. 79.10.249) Portrait statue of Claudia Antonia Tatiana shown as a priestess of Aphrodite. It was discovered in several pieces behind the Odeon. Claudia Antonia Tatiana wears the ritual headdress of a priestess, consisting of a crown decorated with medallion busts. Her hair is arranged in the fashion of Roman Severan princesses, with large ribbed bandeaux com-

134. General view of the Hall of Aphrodite.

ing down to the level of her shoulders and drawn up into a flat chignon on the nape of her neck. A child (Eros?) (its feet are still attached to the base) was by her right side. The statue is signed on its base by Alexander, son of Zenon (see fig. 104).

93. (E. 62.62, 63.63 M. 79.10.250) Colossal statue of Aphrodite of Aphrodisias, which echoes the type of her cult statue probably created in the Hellenistic period. She is shown veiled wearing the *ependytes*, an outer garment that envelops her body which goes over a tunic and is divided into five registers. At breast level, the first one forms an ornamental plate with a wavy design decorated by a crescent-shaped pendant. In the second register, the Three Graces, the goddess' companions, are portrayed between the busts of two divinities, Zeus and Hera. Below, the Sun (Helios) and the Moon (Selene) are separated

by a column. The fourth register depicts animals and sea divinities, thereby alluding to the goddess' origin in the sea, while the fifth register shows three winged Erotes, two of whom are offering a libation at an altar, while a third one is holding a torch upside down symbolising the underworld. All these registers refer to the different roles of the goddess whose powers extended everywhere, as in the case of other Anatolian and Oriental nature goddesses.

94. (E. 64.221, 222 M. 79.10.251) Portrait statue of Diogenes as a priest of Aphrodite. Datable to the late second century. He is a noble-looking figure wrapped in the *himation* in the manner of Greek orators. On top of his thick head of hair sits a tall diadem surmounted by ten miniature busts: the central bust represents Aphrodite while those on the sides are of members of the Antonine and

135. Head of Apollo. From Baths of Hadrian.

136. Full-length portrait statue of a Constantinian priest. From the Odeon.

137. *Head of a Constantinian portrait statue of a priest. From the Theatre.*

138. *Full-length portrait statue of Claudia Antonia Tatiana signed by Alexander, son of Zenon (early third century. Found in portico behind the Odeon).*

140. *Colossal, symbolic representation of the People of Aphrodisias (**Demos**) with its inscribed base. Later first century.*

139. *Colossal statue of the cult image of Aphrodite of Aphrodisias.*

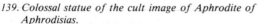

Severan imperial families. Indeed, the priests of Aphrodite were apparently also involved in the Imperial cult.

95. (E. 70.252, 630, M. 79.10.252) This colossal statue of Demos, personification of the People of Aphrodisias, comes from the theatre and stands on its original inscribed base. Several slight distortions of its face and body suggest that it must have been placed in a high niche in the stage façade. Late first cent. A.D..

96. (E. 66.270 M. 79.10.253) Large portrait head of a priestess of Aphrodite, found in the Baths of Hadrian. The head must have belonged to a draped statue. The diadem is decorated with stars and was completed by an additional element inserted into the hole on the crown of the head. First half of the second century A.D..

141. *Head of full-length portrait statue of L. Antonius Dometinus Diogenes, as priest of Aphrodite and of the Imperial cult (late second century.). Found in the portico behind the Odeon*

142. *Head of priest of Aphrodite. Later first century. From the Odeon.*

97. (E. 63.55 M. 79.10.254) Portrait of a priest of Aphrodite, recognisable by his double fillet crown, which carries miniature busts of Aphrodite framed by two imperial ones. End of the first century A.D..

98. (E. 66.269 M. 79.10.255) Large head of Aphrodite, derived from the classical model with the knot of hair (*krobylos*) on the crown of the head.

Opposite the cult-statue in the centre of the hall:

99. (E. 71.153 M. 79.10.256) Relief bust of the Aphrodite of Aphrodisias, veiled and wearing a fillet headband made of laurel leaves and surmounted by a tall crown of towers with a floral motif at the front. The bust is shown wearing the upper part of her usual garment (*ependytes*) with scalloped edges and a crescent-shaped pendant.

100. (E. 74. 291 M. 79.10.257) Colossal head of Aphrodite, from the north Portico of Tiberius. The elongated features of the face, its smile and symmetrical hairstyle give this head an archaistic appearance fashionable under Hadrian (117-138 A.D.).

After leaving the Hall of Aphrodite, one passes through the entrance hall again:

Against the corner pillar:

101. (E. 77.1 M. 79.10.258) Male statuette probably of the god Asklepios, draped in a *himation*. He was leaning on a stick.

On the left, near the window leading to the interior courtyard:

102. (E. 71.363, 72.48 M. 79.10.259) Victory carrying a trophy. Over-lifesize. Discovered in the middle of the theatre stage. It had a matching statue found unfortunately badly battered, and whose torso is in the museum garden. The figure is remarkable for the liveliness of its movement and the elegance of its head. The trophy which she is carrying consists of a pole decorated with enemy spoils (breastplates) and is the symbol of military victory. First cent. B.C..

103. (E. 70.506 M. 79.10.260) Female head, found in the Theatre, with headband. The inspired expression on her face suggests that she may be a Muse.

By the museum administrative wing along the left wall:

104. (E. 67. 213-314, 68.178 M. 79.10.261) Relief figure of Victory. From the Theatre. Its head was added separately, as was its right arm. The goddess wears the *peplos* and a scarf slung across her shoulder.

105. (M. 79,10.262) Small torso belonging to a herm, possibly part of a balustrade. The muscle structure echoes proportions of Archaic sculpture.

Also in the corridor leading to the museum official wing, the following can be seen:

106. (E. 65.236 M. 79.10.263) Head of a young satyr playing the flute. Found in the Baths of Hadrian. His brow is knitted with the effort of playing, his cheeks puffed out. There are traces of his playing instrument on his lips. Certain details suggest that the head belonged to a replica of a Hellenistic type showing a satyr leaning against a tree and playing a flute.

143. Relief bust of Aphrodite of Aphrodisias. From the theatre stage decoration.

By the entrance hall, against the west wall:

107. (M. 79.10.264) Large nude torso of male divinity or hero found in 1904-5 during the Gaudin excavations of the Baths of Hadrian. The *chlamys* fastened on the right shoulder and traces of an attribute suggests a statue of Hermes, the messenger god.

108. (E. 63.54, 56 M. 79.10.265) Headless female statue wearing a finely pleated tunic buttoned over the arms and a mantle which enfolds her hips and her left arm. She may be a female divinity or a prominent private person.

To the right of the museum exit:

109. (M. 79.10.266) Mosaic found in a dwelling to the east of the Odeon, and representing the goddess Aphrodite, nude, her hair in a chignon held with ribbons, and wearing earrings. She is standing among flowers, her right arm stretched out. The inscription refers to "Aphrodite".

Interior Courtyard

Walking around the courtyard in an anti-clockwise direction, from the right, one can see:

110. (M. 79.10.267) Headless male statue portrayed in the stance and drapery of an orator, wearing the *himation*.

111. (M. 79.10.268) Sarcophagus decorated with garlands. From the south necropolis. The box of the sarcophagus is decorated on three faces and its lid shaped like a gabled roof. There are side projections which enabled the lid to be lifted with ropes so as to place it on the box. There are also holes from the metal clamps which served to close the sarcophagus after burial had taken place. Inside the box can be seen small brackets at the corners. These were used to rest wooden planks that made it possible to place at least two bodies on top of one another. The front of the sarcophagus is decorated with garlands supported at both ends by two figures of Victory holding palms. In the middle, two male figures dressed in the attire of orators support the cluster of garlands, in the curves of which are three busts. Since robbers of the tomb where the sarcophagus was found damaged it, only the toga-clad bust of the figure on the right has survived. The hairstyle of the female figure in the centre allows us to date the sarcophagus to the middle of the third century. The young man on the right with sideburns and short hair is wearing a simple cloak. The figures are clearly members of the same family which commissioned this sarcophagus. Erased inscriptions visible on the face of the box imply that the sarcophagus was reused at least once.

112. (M. 79.10.269) Relief showing a male figure dressed as a traveller, or a shepherd, leaning on a stick.

113. (E. 70. 219 M. 79.10.270) Colossal draped female statue. Found in the south end of the Portico of Tiberius. The distinctive drapery of the mantle is reminiscent of the drapery of one of the Muses on the relief by Archelaos of Priene (British Museum). However, this figure was undoubtedly a goddess or an empress.

114. (M. 79.10.271) Fragment of a relief depicting a figure wrapped in a cloak (Perhaps belonging to the Zoilos monument).

Against the wall, to the left:

115. (M. 79.10.272) Sarcophagus box

144. Interior courtyard. View with sarcophagus and draped female figure (to left).

representing the deceased surrounded by female figures, some of which may be Muses. He is wearing the *himation* clasping his wife's hand (to the right). The other female figures are dressed differently: one of them is accompanied by a small child, perhaps a relative of the dead man. The theme of Muses surrounding a dead man often reflected a belief common in Roman society of the second century according to which men who, during their lifetime, had cultivated the arts and letters and had thus elevated their minds, were rewarded in the afterlife.

116. (M. 79.10.273) Cylindrical altar decorated with bulls' heads (*bucrania*) supporting a garland made of ivy berries, pine cones, bay-tree branches and hanging grapes. The garland is tied with large ribbons.

117. (M. 79.10.274) Male statue found east of the Odeon. The figure is draped in the *himation*.

By the elevated section of the north courtyard:

118. (M. 79.10.275, 276, 277) Three blocks of a frieze with garlands and masks. From the southwest corner of the Portico of Tiberius. The heads are theatre masks: divinities such as Pan and Dionysos, satyrs, old men, young male and female theatre leads.

119. (M. 79.10.278) Fragment of sarcophagus found near the west gate of the city. The box decorated with columns and pediments belongs to the type known as "Asiatic" or "Sidamara". A mythological scene is portrayed between two columns: in the foreground a small child, probably Herakles, grasping snakes, is surrounded by several Olympian gods and goddesses Among them, the helmeted Athena, is identifiable.

In the recess of the window to the right:

120. (M. 79.10.279) Cylindrical altar decorated with *bucrania* supporting garlands with pendants of pomegranates and grapes. It bears a cross carved on it in Christians times.

121. (M. 79.10.280) Sarcophagus box with figures between columns. In front, the deceased, draped in the *himation* pose, is flanked by four female figures (Muses). On the right short side, are another Muse and a draped woman: on the left, two draped figures, perhaps relatives.

122. (M. 79.10.281) Female statue found during the 1904-5 Gaudin excavations near the east city wall. Its drapery suggests a Trajanic date. It was indeed known as the drapery "of the initiate" because figures thus represented often carried a bunch of poppies and ears-of-corn that symbolised their initiation into the Eleusinian Mysteries.

Near the door leading to the Display Case Gallery:

123. (M. 79.10.282) Sarcophagus box decorated with garlands, supported by Erotes and figures of Victory at the corners. In the curve of the garlands are mythological motifs: in the centre, Eros embracing Psyche, and to the left and right, Ganymede carried off by Zeus in the form of an eagle. These scenes obviously symbolised the soul's access to celestial happiness.

124. (E. 74.290 M. 79.10.283) Relief found in the west wall of the city. It depicts an actor dressed as an Oriental, wearing a Phrygian cap and holding a tragic mask. The actor may have been playing the role of Paris or of a Trojan in a tragedy based on the cycle of the Trojan War.

In the centre of the courtyard:

125. (M. 79.10.284) Cylindrical altar found in the front court of the Baths of Hadrian, decorated with *bucrania*, garlands and ribbons. The garlands swing under the head of a Medusa, that of an old man (possibly the god Pan) and a rosette.

126. (E. 60.194 M. 79.10.285) Cylindrical altar featuring garlands and masks hangings from ribbon bows. All that remains of the decoration is the mask of a young laughing boy, wearing a tall head of hair (*onchos*) typical of tragic masks.

Decorating the fountain on the west side of the courtyard:

127. Recumbent statue of a young river god, wearing reeds in his hair and holding a stalk in his hand. The lower part of the body is draped. The god was leaning against an urn which symbolised the source of the river. The statue was part of the decoration of the façade of the Agora Gate at the east end of the Portico of Tiberius (currently still being excavated) transformed into a fountain-house or *nymphaeum* in the fifth century, A.D..

Outside and around the museum, visitors can also see various sculptures scattered in the grounds.

In front of the museum, along the façade to the left, are three sarcophagi of the garland type very frequently found Aphrodisias.

The first sarcophagus (M. 78.7.83) consists of spirally fluted columns supporting garlands, and a cartouche inscribed with the name of the

145. Interior courtyard. Reclining statue of a river god.

146. Backgardens of museum, with mask and garland frieze fragments.

147. *Sarcophagus in front gardens of museum.*

deceased, Dionysios Diogenianos. In the curve of the garlands, Medusa heads and the rape of Ganymede are recognisable.

The second sarcophagus, of which only the box remains features garlands, figures of Victory and Erotes as supports, and as medallions, eagles, masks of Medusa and satyrs on the short ends of the box.

The third sarcophagus (against the north façade of the museum) is also decorated with Erotes and garlands, only on the front and short ends. The back is roughly carved, with only the outlines of its decoration since the sarcophagus was placed in a recess or against a wall.

Other similar sarcophagi can be seen in the eastern part of the museum garden. On the lawn, near the southeast corner are several reliefs decorated with garlands and masks,

that come from the *Sebasteion*'s north portico where they served as bases for reliefs depicting the peoples conquered by Augustus.

Outside the entrance of the museum, to the left as one leaves, stands a large sarcophagus (M. 79.2.114 A, B) of a priest of Aphrodite. The deceased, accompanied by his wife, is shown in the centre of the front panel. Both husband and wife wear the medallion-bust crowns of the priests of Aphrodite. To their right are the goddesses Demeter and Kore, who symbolised resurrection, and a funerary spirit leaning against an upside-down torch. (*Hypnos? Thanatos?*). To their left, Hermes, conductor of souls, and the god Hades, husband of Kore and master of the underworld are identifiable. The sarcophagus may be dated to the second half of the second century A.D. (see fig. 99).

Opposite this last sarcophagus, is another

more, original one featuring a front panel framed with garland and bearing a long inscription, and two facing busts of the deceased, undoubtedly husband and wife.

Along the south façade of the museum, to the right as one leaves, an unfinished sarcophagus with Erotes, figures of Victory and garlands can be seen. The decoration was carved using the drill and leaving rows of holes. The tondo busts of the deceased were merely outlined while the masks on the sides were finished: Dionysos and Silvanus are on the left, Silvanus and Pan on the right.

In the area planted with rose-bushes running along the south façade of the museum are aligned (from east to west) several draped torsos: the first belongs to the second Victory from the Theatre (cf. no.102). The second belonged to a woman draped in the manner of an *orans* (praying figure) and was found in the neighbouring ancient city of Herakleia Salbake (mod. Karahisar). The third one is a male torso draped in a *himation*.

At the corner of the garden and the path leading to the core of the site is a large funerary stele with a pediment crowned with palmettes. An inscription giving the names and qualities of the deceased was carved above the figures of Victory. These frame a female figure who carries various attributes, and probably represents a Pantheic Fortuna.

On the west lawn, a draped male torso, a statuette of a Romano-Byzantine magistrate wearing a *chlamys* and a female torso of the *Pudicitia* type can be seen.

The box of a sarcophagus nearby with a large inscribed *tabula ansata* on its front is unfinished with outlines of garlands and other stylised forms corresponding to figures.

148. Mask and garland decorated frieze fragment. From Portico of Tiberius.

A last torso located near the poplar groves belongs to a replica of the group of Menelaus bringing back the body of Patroclus. This served as a counterpart to the group of Achilles and Penthesilea on the sides of the *frigidarium* pool of the Baths of Hadrian. The accentuated contorsion of the torso, the sleeveless tunic (*exomis*) recall similar details of the famous "Pasquino" torso in the Piazza Navona in Rome which belonged to a similar group.

In the poplar groves to the west of the museum are many fragments of sarcophagi: some are decorated with garlands, Erotes and figures of Victory, others with Muses, or belong to "Asiatic" types.

In a small garden across from the back entrance of the museum, are two sarcophagus lids with figures lying on a bed (*kline*) and various capitals from the site.

Following the path in the garden behind the museum, one may see several gladiatorial stelai (offered as ex-votos), and which depict such men dressed for combat.

To the right, near the rear entrance to the museum the top back half of a colossal male statue, an element of balustrade decorated with an Eros figure and a garland sarcophagus are exhibited.

Along the north wall that encloses the museum garden, near the director's lodgings are several large inscribed plaques bearing parts of the Edict of Prices, promulgated in 301 A.D. by the emperor Diocletian, and setting prices for all products, foodstuffs, spices, perfumes, materials, drugs, marbles as well as services and transportation.

Above these panels and all along the top of the north wall are frieze blocks decorated with garlands and heads; these belong for the most part, to the large Portico of Tiberius of the agora complex of the city. The heads represent an astonishing variety of faces and masks: divinities such as Dionysos, Pan, Selene, Zeus, and Athena; mythological characters, including satyrs and Silenus as well as tragic or comic theatre masks of old men, leading actors, heroines, courtesans, slaves and servants.

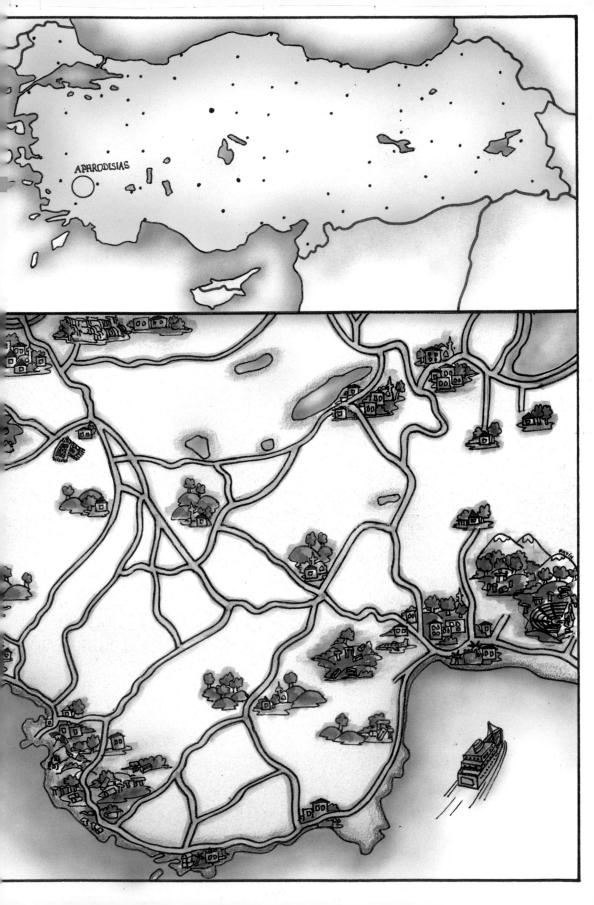

SELECT GLOSSARY

acropolis: Citadel, or fortified height of an ancient Greek city.

agora: Market-place or area of an ancient Greek city (equivalent of Latin *forum*).

Amazon: Mythological people of female warriors usually located on the fringes of the ancient world. Amazons are frequently represented in classical art fighting Greeks, hence the term 'Amazonomachy' (lit. 'Amazon fight') applied to such combat scenes.

Anatolia: Essentially modern geographic and archaeological term used to refer to the Asiatic portion of Turkey.

apodyterium: Dressing, or changing room in a Roman bath.

Archaic: Adjective used in connection with pre-classical art and architecture, i.e. from the seventh century to ca. 500 B.C.

Asia: In Roman historical context, province including most of western Turkey (or Anatolia).

atrium: Central hall of a Roman private house. In an early Christian church, it refers to a front court usually framed by colonnades.

basilica: A structure, long and rectangular, whose plan consisted of a central hall, or nave, flanked by side aisles and often terminating in an apse at one end. In Roman times, the basilica was used for administrative and judicial purposes.

Bessi: People of Thrace.

bouleuterion: Small theatre-like structure used for the meetings of a city council (*boulé*). Essentially similar to an odeon.

calidarium: Hot room of a Roman bath.

cavea: Seating area of a theatre: lower (*ima cavea*) and upper (*summa cavea*) sections.

cella: Enclosed central shrine, or chamber, of a Greek or Roman temple where the statue of the divinity stood.

Centaurs: Mythological, wild, part-horse, part-human creatures. Fought against the Lapiths, a people of Thessaly in northern Greece. These fights are frequent motifs of classical art, hence the term 'Centauromachy' (lit. 'Centaur fight).

conch: Semicircular niche, generally featuring a half dome. Hence, *triconch* referring to a cluster of three conches, or a room featuring a trefoil plan.

conistra: In Roman times, deepened area between stage and *cavea*, roughly equivalent to the Greek orchestra of classical times,, used as an arena for gladiatorial and animal fights.

crepis: Stepped platform of a Greek (or Roman) temple.

Dacians: People of the lower Danube basin (today's Roumania).

frigidarium: Cold room of a Roman bath.

Giants: Mythological creatures, offspring of Ge (the Earth) and Uranus. Represented usually in ancient art as snake-legged monsters. Challenged the Olympian Gods and attempted to overthrow them. Such fights are frequent motifs in later ancient art (especially Hellenistic), hence the term 'Gigantomachy' (lit. Giants' fight) referring to scenes of battle between Gods and Giants.

Hellenistic: Adjective referring to the period following the death of Alexander the Great (323 B.C.) up to Octavian's (later Augustus') control of the whole Mediterranean basin (31 B.C., Battle of Actium), marking the spread of Greek culture and civilisation beyond the limits of Greece proper.

heroon: Small shrine, or sanctuary for a hero, an important person or a semi-deified individual.

höyük or hüyük: Turkish word referring to an artificial mound created over centuries by successive habitations consisting of mud brick construction.

in situ: (Lat.) In place; at its original location.

logeion: Platform, or podium in a Hellenistic-type theatre.

mappa: Handkerchief used for waving by presiding official to signal the start of games and festivity.

nymphaeum: In Roman times, a monumental fountain-house with running water.

octastyle: Featuring eight columns on its façade.

odeon: Small theatre-like structure, usually roofed, where more intimate performances, plays or musical shows were held.

oecus: In Roman houses, a banqueting room, or in more general terms, an important room in any other building.

opus sectile: Pavement consisting of varied, mostly geometric stone or marble tiles of different colours forming distinctive patterns.

palaestra: Area for athletic exercises.

parodos: Side entrance to the orchestra, or stage, of a Greek or Roman theatre.

peristyle: Colonnade, or ring of columns surrounding a building (or an open court, or garden).

proskenion: Front portion of a theatre stage.

Sebasteion: From Sebastos (Gr. for Lat. Augustus). Place or shrine complex dedicated to the cult of the deified Augustus and/or other emperors.

stoa: Covered portico featuring a colonnade in front and a wall at its back.

sudatorium: Sweating room in a Roman bath.

temenos: Sacred precinct or enclosure within which a temple, or group of shrines, were located.

tepidarium: Lukewarm hall in a Roman bath.

BIBLIOGRAPHY

1. *Early Travel Accounts and Reports.*

   Antiquities of Ionia, Society of Dilettanti, London, III, 1840, pls. I-XXIV.

   Ch. Texier, *Description de l'Asie Mineure*, Paris, III, 1849, 149 ff., pls, 150 ff.

   L. de Laborde, *Voyage de l'Asie Mineure*, Paris, 1872, pl. 53.

2. *General Accounts*

   R. Vagts, *Aphrodisias in Karien*, Diss., Hamburg, 1920.

   G. Becatti, in *Enciclopedia dell'Arte Antica, Classica e Orientale* Rome, 1958, I, 109-115.

3. *Early Excavations*

   M. Collignon, in *Revue de l'Art Ancien et Moderne*, 19 (1906), 33 ff.

   G. Jacopi, in *Monumenti Antichi* 38 (1939-40).

4. *Sculpture*

   M.F. Squarciapino, *La Scuola di Afrodisia*, Rome, 1943.

5. *Inscriptions*

   Th. Reinach, in *Revue des Etudes Grecques*, 19 (1906), 79-150 and 205-298.

   W.M. Calder and J.M.R. Cormack. *Monumenta Asiae Minoris Antiqua. VIII: Monuments from Lycaonia, the Pisido-Phrygian Border, Aphrodisias*, Manchester, 1962, 72-160.

RECENT BIBLIOGRAPHY

K.T. Erim, *Aphrodisias. City of Venus Aphrodite*, London- New York 1986.

J. de la Genière, K.T. Erim, *Aphrodisias de Carie, Colloque de l'Université de bille III*, 13 novembre 1986, Edition Recherche sur les civilisation, Paris 1987.

Also:

K.T. Erim, in *Supplemento. Enciclopedia dell'Arte Antica, Orientale*, Rome, 1973, 9-17.

K.T. Erim, "Aphrodisias" in *Princeton Encyclopedia of Classical Sites*, Princeton, 1976, 68-70.

G. Bean, *Turkey Beyond the Maeander*, London 1980, 188-198.

J.M. Reynolds, *Aphrodisias and Rome*, London 1982.

M.S. Joukowsky, *Prehistoric Aphrodisias*, Providence, R.I. and Louvain-la-Neuve, 1986.

J.M. Reynolds and R.F. Tannenbaum, *Jews and Godfearers at Aphrodisias*, Proceedings of the Cambridge Philological Society, suppl. vol. 1986.

C.W. Roueché with, M. Reynolds, *Aphrodisias in Late Antiquity*, London, 1989.

BAZAAR 54 ISTANBUL
Nuruosmaniye

Quality
Reliability & Service

Carpet

Jewellery

Leather

Souvenir